THE
NATIONAL PARKS
OF THE
UNITED STATES

LUIS·A·BOLIN

THE

Translated from the Spanish by Herbert Weinstock

NEW YORK 1962

ALFRED·A·KNOPF

OF THE

NATIONAL
PARKS
UNITED STATES

L. C. catalog card number: 62-8690

THIS IS A BORZOI BOOK,

PUBLISHED BY ALFRED A. KNOPF, INC.

FIRST AMERICAN EDITION

Originally published in Spain as *Parques Nacionales Norteamericanos* by Editora Nacional, Madrid, in 1960.

I wish to thank the National Park Service for the photographs of the parks reproduced here, and for much kindness received during my visits to the parks.

L. A. B.

FOREWORD

I<small>T WAS</small> after I had been in twenty national parks—four in Spain, five in Canada, and eleven in the United States—that the idea of writing something about the parks in the United States first occurred to me. Nature is beautiful in many places; in certain areas of the North American continent it is exceptionally beautiful. But as far as I know there is nothing comparable, anywhere, to what is being done in the United States of America to preserve the wonders of nature in so many national parks and to make them accessible to all, young or old, nimble or sluggish. It was when I saw Americans in their national parks that I began to think about a book that might be of value to countries with territories just as beautiful, but with only vague notions as to what should be done to maintain their charm.

In the United States, apart from the question of whether, on principle, other national parks should be established, there is a feeling at present that those which already exist are being exploited, that their resources are being developed and used to a degree which is incompatible with the duty of preserving their primeval qualities for future generations. I sympathize with this feeling but do not share it; provided that people can be educated to use the parks properly and restrained from misusing them, the parks are for the people. It may be frightening to learn that in 1961 seventy-eight million of our contemporaries visited American national parks. But once we break down this total—and it should be broken down so that its real meaning can be grasped—the result tends to be reassuring, for it corresponds to a daily average of little more than seven thousand visitors in each of the thirty national parks. Although the figure is certainly higher during the summer, the parks seem big enough to hold these numbers.

Similar doubts and premonitions assailed some people in Spain when that country was being organized for the tremendous tourist influx it is now receiving. This influx, incidentally, benefits the economy of Spain by some five hundred million dollars a year—not to mention the good will resulting from a firsthand acquaintance with Spain. Now that much is being done to attract foreign visitors to the United States, it may be assumed that no effort will be spared to direct some of their interest to the national parks. There, besides enjoying great natural beauty, they will see what the National Park Service has done to make the parks appreciated and understood. They will also see Americans at their best, behaving as they should and accompanied by their equally well-behaved children, who are sometimes fascinating to watch. What the mere fact of being there means to them is quite obvious. You have only to look at their faces, filled with wonder and ecstasy, thrilled beyond belief by the vision of what God has created, for man to see and enjoy.

A Spaniard who knows his country rapidly acquires a feeling of friendliness and familiarity for the vast scenic beauties of the United States; in his own land he also has distant horizons, limpid skies and immense stretches, high sierras, towering crags, and rushing torrents. In other parts of Europe the scenery is different; rarely can it be compared to American landscapes, the grandeur of which is imposing enough to overawe some. It failed to intimidate the Spaniards who were the first white men to set eyes or even feet on eighteen of the territories upon which, in the course of time, national parks have been established in the United States. They took it in their stride, possibly imagining that the world was smaller than it really was and that, because it was round, as one of them had just proved, behind that blue range which would soon hide the setting sun and toward which they were walking they might perhaps stumble upon some part of their beloved country. They had left it in a spirit of conquest and endeavor; to return to it eventually was the greatest reward they could hope for.

For a period of fifteen years, in Spain, I had three national big-game preserves under my care: the Coto Nacional de Monteses, with *capra pyrenaica Victoriae,* or Spanish ibex, in the Sierra de Gredos, northwest of Ávila and not far from Madrid; the Coto Nacional de Rebecos, with *rupicapra pyrenaica,* or chamois, in the Picos de Europa, the craggy limestone peaks of Asturias and Santander; and another Coto Nacional de Monteses, with *capra hispanica,* a variety of Spanish ibex, in Sierra Blanca de Ojén, not far from Ronda, in the province of Málaga, and overlooking the Straits of Gibraltar. These three territories are as different from each other as they could possibly be; as big-game preserves they rank with the finest in the world. My task in each was the same: conservation of the natural resources indispensable for the growth of the species that live in them, so that sportsmen from all lands might stalk them in strictly limited numbers and in accordance with well-defined regulations guaranteeing their survival. During those years I hunted in Spain from the Pyrenees to the mouth of the Guadalquivir River; later I shot big game in Alaska and in the

Sangre de Cristo Range, facing the Great Divide; I am an honorary member of the Shikar Club in London and of the Conseil Internationale de la Chasse in Paris. Some of the best hours of my life have been spent gazing at distant landscapes while waiting for game or for the horse that would take me on the long trek homewards. I love the scenic panoramas of America and of American national parks and feel a deep admiration for the National Park Service and the work it carries out for the parks and for the people to whom the parks belong. I hope that this book—the first of its kind, I am told, to be written by a non-American—may foster in other countries the creation or organization of national parks modeled on those of which the people of the United States have good reason to be proud.

LUIS A. BOLIN

CONTENTS

ILLUSTRATIONS

xi

THE
NATIONAL PARKS
OF THE
UNITED STATES

A short walk from a good road in Big Bend National Park leads to the spot where the waters of Terlingua Creek meet the Rio Grande in Santa Elena Canyon. The hills in the background are in Mexico.

I

The Beginnings

IN THE United States, public authority has set aside immense territorial and aquatic reserves to preserve their distinctive characteristics for all time and assure their use to present and future generations. The National Park Service of the United States lists 170 such preserves, not including animal life refuges, national forests—with, respectively, about 44,450,000 acres and about 173,-000,000 acres—or the numerous areas of a similar nature under the jurisdiction of the fifty states.

Most important of these areas for their extraordinary interest and beauty and the admirable manner in which they are administered are the thirty national parks that are the subject of this book. What has been accomplished in these parks is so significant and of such scientific and cultural value that it justifies careful study. No other country has improved upon it or achieved anything comparable. The vast regions involved—their area reaches 31,000 square miles—contain some of the most majestic natural scenery of the world in which we live.

THE FIRST NATIONAL PARKS

Large areas were first set aside as national parks during the last third of the nineteenth century. Yellowstone was established in 1872; Sequoia and Yosemite followed in 1890, Mount Rainier in 1899. The seven youngest national parks were created between 1940 and 1961.

These dates indicate the continuing strength of a movement that arose about ninety years ago and now enlists the enthusiastic support both of public opinion and of the government of the United States. The park system has grown since 1872 as a result of measures adopted by successive Congresses in answer to insistent popular demands stimulated by an understanding and influential press. In 1916, when ten national parks had been established and were in operation, their administration and preservation were confided to the National Park Service created by Congress on August 25 of that year and assigned to the Department of the Interior. The Park Service also was assigned the national monuments, which often differ notably from units so designated in other countries, and also differ greatly among themselves. Some of them resemble the parks; most are entirely distinct from them.

THE PARK SERVICE

The fundamental mission of the Park Service is the conservation of landscape, natural and historic objects, and wildlife so that they shall be preserved for the use of future generations. Inside the parks, the Service lays out and builds roads and trails and sets up camping zones. Such other necessary facilities as hotels, inns, cabins, and shelters, as well as public transportation, are contracted for with private concessionaires. The Federal government inspects and regulates them, but does not take a direct part in running them.

A well-uniformed, well-trained, courteous, and eminently effective personnel represents the Service, protects the parks and monuments against fires and acts of barbarism, directs traffic, and carries out technical missions of great interest. Naturalists and historians connected with the Service and specializing in the subjects discussed give pleasant, instructive talks to visitors and also act as guides to the most notable sites. In almost all the national parks and national monuments this extremely useful work is well complemented by museums.

In conformity with the belief that those who use a public preserve should contribute to the cost of maintaining it, small charges usually (but not invariably) are made for guide services and for the admission of vehicles and their passengers. The general rules to be observed in these zones are dictated by good sense and good manners; they have been formulated in the interest of the areas themselves and of their visitors. The most recent version of the principal rules in effect in the national parks is contained in the following pages.

The National Park Service is a bureau of the Department of the Interior, and as such has its head office in Washington, D. C.

It is divided into two sections, one for projects, the other for construction, and has six regional offices, which are located in Philadelphia, Richmond, St. Louis, Omaha, Santa Fe, and San Francisco. Each of these has a director in charge of the parks and monuments in his district and of the works carried out in them. A superintendent administers each preserve and the personnel assigned to it. The specific functions of the Service are co-ordinated in special sections: Interpretation, Conservation and Protection, Lands, Concessions, and Project Control.

The Park Service personnel performs its duties with high spirit and exemplary zeal. "If we remain faithful to the ideals that inspire us," Robert Sterling Young, first Executive Secretary of the National Parks Association said, "our institution can come to be one of the noblest organizations functioning on the Earth." Stephen Mather, first Director of the Service, said: "The parks already established tell us what must be the rules for creating others in the future. If we respect those rules, we will neither create too many parks nor lower the quality of those already in existence."

Certain sites of chiefly historic interest—battlefields, commemorative zones, military parks, and the urban parks of Washington, D. C.—also are assigned to the National Park Service.

PROGRESSIVE DEVELOPMENT

The United States already had fifteen national parks and an efficient Service administering them when increasing need began to be felt for rules to regulate their use and assure the integrity and uniformity of the system. As first drafted by Stephen Mather and Franklin K. Lane, who had been Secretary of the Interior shortly before, these rules were supported by numerous organizations.

Set forth in 1923, they constituted the basis for the policies to be followed in establishing future preserves and maintaining their high prestige. In 1943 the National Parks Association, which has contributed to their high quality, formulated the rules, completing this task the following year, when all the parks were in existence except that of the Everglades, created in extreme southern Florida in 1947, that in the Virgin Islands, established in 1956, and Haleakala National Park, which was separated from Hawaii National Park in 1961.

Early in 1957, the Association completed drafting a revision of the definitions and rules applicable to these preserves. It then issued them in a version reflecting criticisms made by the Park Service and by private citizens and authorized groups since the first national park was created in 1872. Because of the continuing interest of these definitions and the innovations they embody, I reproduce them here verbatim.

A NATIONAL POLICY

FOR THE ESTABLISHMENT AND PROTECTION
OF NATIONAL PARKS AND MONUMENTS

This declaration of policy is a revision of the standards originally developed by the Camp Fire Club of America and endorsed by nearly a hundred organizations, including the National Parks Association. Offered by the Association to help crystallize fundamental ideals, it is based on the thinking of the National Park Service and a number of organizations and individuals through the years since the establishment of the first national park in 1872.

DEFINITIONS

National Parks

National Parks are spacious land and water areas of nation-wide interest established as inviolable sanctuaries for the permanent preservation of scenery, wilderness, and native fauna and flora in their natural condition. National parks are composed of wilderness essentially in a primeval condition, of areas of scenic magnificence, and of a wide variety of features. Their unexcelled quality and unique inspirational beauty distinguish them from all other areas, and make imperative their protection, through Act of Congress, for human enjoyment, education and inspiration for all time.

National Nature Monuments

National Nature Mounments * are established to preserve specific natural phenomena of such significance that their protection is in the national interest; they are the finest examples of their kind, and are given the same inviolate federal protection as the national parks. While there may be wilderness and scenery in some of the nature monuments, their primary purpose is to protect geological formations, biological features and other significant examples of nature's handiwork. The monuments differ from the parks in that they usually do not have such a wide variety of outstanding features. They may be set aside by Act of Congress, but more often they are established by presidential proclamation, under authority of the *Antiquities Act* of 1906.

---

* The term "national nature monument," while not official, is used here for the sake of clarity to show that the monuments under consideration are those established to preserve the wonders of nature.

8

The magic of Bryce Canyon is best appreciated by following, on foot or on horseback, the trails that are a feature of this national park.

APPLICATION OF PRINCIPLES

1. National Parks and Monuments Are of National Importance

An area is judged to merit national park or monument status and commitment to federal care by the degree of its value and interest to the nation as a whole. Every proposal for the establishment of a new national park or monument should be carefully examined lest it lead to the admission of an area of lesser importance, and thus form a precedent for the future admission of inferior areas which would dilute the splendor of the system. The sanctuaries should differ as widely as possible from one another, and represent a broad range of features of supreme quality.

2. Adequate Area Is Required

National parks and national nature monuments are set aside for the enjoyment, scientific study and permanent preservation, in a natural state, of the native plant and animal life and other features within them. Each should be a comprehensive unit embracing sufficient area for effective administration, and where the fauna and flora are of major significance, should include adequate year-round habitat.

3. Protection Is Based on Scientific and Esthetic Values

Federal guardianship of national parks and national nature monuments involves sound scientific research looking to the protection of wilderness, and plant and animal life and other natural features, and it recognizes those great intangible values of inspirational beauty that make their protection imperative. The highest scientific and inspirational quality of the areas are (*sic*) the special, unique values of the national parks and national nature monuments. Visitors enjoyment is based on seeing and experiencing wilderness and the wonders and beauties of nature, without interference from man-made distractions. Future generations have the right to enjoy these sanctuaries unimpaired by present-day use as required by the Act of 1916, establishing the National Park Service.

4. *Congress Intends Enjoyment of Unimpaired Nature*

When Congress adopted the Act of 1916, establishing the National Park Service, it made that agency of the government the guardian of national parks and monuments, and it charged the Service with the responsibility to *conserve the scenery and the natural and historic objects and the wildlife therein and to provide for the enjoyment of the same in such a manner and by such means as will leave them unimpaired for the enjoyment of future generations.* Public enjoyment of the natural features of the national parks and national nature monuments is their basic reason for being; the areas are, in fact, living museums. Necessary facilities for visitors should, therefore, be constructed with the least possible alteration of the natural scene.

5. *Private Inholdings Are Being Acquired*

The acquisition of privately owned lands within national parks and national nature monuments is imperative to facilitate administration and protection, and to prevent intrusion of undesirable developments and activities on them. Such acquisition is being carried out as rapidly as feasible.

6. *Wilderness Preservation Is Vital*

Wilderness is one of the most significant attributes of the national parks and the national nature monuments, and because it is fragile and irreplaceable, it is kept inviolate and is accessible only by trail.

7. *Commercial Uses Are Destructive*

The national policy recognizes no use of national parks and national nature monuments for commercial purposes, because such use would alter natural conditions and scenery, which these areas have been established to preserve. Every alteration of the natural

Crater Lake National Park, shown in the map stretched before a National Park Service ranger, is partly covered by dense forests that require ceaseless vigilance to prevent fires from spreading.

landscape, however slight, by such activities as logging, mining, grazing, airport and railroad construction, or damming of watercourses, is a direct violation of a fundamental principle of national park management.

8. Amusement Attractions Are Inconsistent

National parks and national nature monuments are not resorts or amusement centers. The introduction of incongruous recreational features diminishes visitors' enjoyment of the basic character of the sanctuaries. Resort amusement facilities, such as golf courses, swimming pools, ski lifts, tramways, skating rinks, tennis courts and speedboats, abundantly available elsewhere, destroy wilderness atmosphere, and defeat the purpose of visitors who wish to derive inspiration from contact with pristine nature.

9. Interpretation Is the Key to Appreciation

Interpretive programs, with museums, adequate literature, visual aids, guided trips and lectures, are based on the natural features of each area, and are given special emphasis by the National Park Service. The Service informs visitors about the purposes of the areas under its care, stimulates respect for the irreplaceable objects of natural and scientific interest, and emphasizes the special significance of the particular area, as well as of the system as a whole. The National Park Service needs adequate funds to employ a sufficient staff of naturalists to serve the rapidly growing number of visitors.

10. Protection of Plants and Animals Is Fundamental

Public shooting of wildlife in national parks and national nature monuments is contrary to the basic principle that these areas are inviolable sanctuaries, and it is prohibited throughout the park and monument system. Whenever scientific research shows that a native species has become so abundant as to endanger its habitat or the survival of another native species, the National Park Service has authority to reduce its numbers. The introduction of non-native species is contrary to the principle that the national parks and monuments are sanctuaries for *native* wildlife.

Sport and commercial fishing are incompatible with the concept that the national parks and monuments are inviolable sanctuaries for native fauna. Commercial fishing is prohibited, or eliminated as soon as possible. So long as sport fishing is legal, streams and lakes are stocked only when natural reproduction fails to provide enough fish for angling, and then only with species native to the area. High country lakes, where fish do not occur naturally, are not stocked.

Indiscriminate cutting of trees and shrubs and mowing of meadows, and the picking and digging of wild flowers and other plants, are contrary to the principle of inviolate protection of nature. At important overlooks along roads and trails, and at locations where people may observe outstanding manifestations of nature, thinning of vegetation sometimes may be necessary, and it is performed under trained supervision. The removal of dead or dying trees that may endanger people in areas of heavy use, also may be required at times, as in campgrounds and picnic areas, or along trails and roads.

11. *Mechanical Noise Is an Adverse Intrusion*

Where airfields and railroad stations exist in national parks and monuments, long-range planning looks toward their removal at the earliest time to sites outside the boundaries. Because outboard motors, speedboats and airplanes are a disturbing influence to those seeking the quiet serenity of nature, as well as detrimental to wildlife, they should be prohibited in national parks and monuments. Low altitude flying over national parks and monuments should be restricted to patroling, forest fire suppression, rescue, and supply service to ranger outposts that are difficult of access.

12. *Roads Are Held to a Minimum*

Only such roads are built in national parks and national nature monuments as are needed to provide access to some of the principal features of the sanctuaries, and to facilitate their protection. Roads are located so they will mar scenery and natural features as little as possible, and they are constructed for leisurely driving and not for speed or commercial traffic.

13. *Buildings Should Be Designed to Blend with Environment*

Buildings within national parks and national nature monuments are designed to be unobtrusive as possible, and to harmonize with their surroundings. They are erected only where necessary for efficient administration and for the convenience of visitors, at locations where they will least interfere with the natural scene or, where feasible and desirable, outside the boundaries of the parks and monuments. Wherever existing facilities detract from important scenic and scientific features, every effort is being made to move them to unobjectionable sites. Long-range planning envisons the eventual removal of many hotels and lodges to sites outside the boundaries.

14. *Concessions Are Only for Necessary Accommodations*

Concessions in national parks and national nature monuments are granted only for the necessary care of visitors, and then in restricted locations; and they are operated so as not to lower the dignity of the sanctuaries. National parks and monuments are not established and maintained to provide local or personal profit, and the installation of crowd-attracting facilities and amusements to increase concessioner revenue, or to bolster local income, is a misuse of these reservations.

15. *National Archeological Monuments Are Similarly Guarded*

National archeological monuments, which are established specifically to protect the structures and other remains of indigenous civilization, are administered under the same principles as set forth herein for the national nature monuments, wherever these are applicable.

16. The Violation of One Park Is a Threat to All

Any infraction of these principles in any national park or monument constitutes a threat to all national parks and monuments.

*   *   *

Notice the frequent repetition in this document of such words as *primeval* and *wilderness*. These are the distinguishing qualifications that the National Parks Association has added to the legal terminology for denominating national parks in the United States. Its deliberate purpose was to isolate the characteristic that it considered essential to any definition of them: the inviolability that they have enjoyed for centuries, the protection that their very isolation has given them against depredations or exploitation by man—the quality, that is, of primeval, pristine wilderness areas which so clearly distinguishes and differentiates them. Almost all the thirty parks now existing in the territory of the United States unquestionably possess these magnificent qualities, in themselves of sufficient weight to defend them from the attacks and criticisms sometimes directed against them by people who do not believe in national values that cannot be measured in terms of political economics.

At the present time, the standards for creation of a new national park substantially conform to the bill of particulars quoted above. The parks established most recently maintain the prestige of those established earlier. They differ from the oldest parks so that the whole System may offer greater variety. But nearly all are of the highest quality. An important point: in theory, at least, areas of sparse or predominantly local interest are never admitted into the National Park System.

The surface of Crater Lake is often unrippled, but the contour of the land encircling the lake rises and falls as gracefully as a wave.

LEGISLATIVE PROCEDURE

Once an area's suitability has been ascertained, the steps toward its formal establishment as a national park begin with the introduction of a bill in Congress. The area is studied by the Committees on Public Lands of both the Senate and the House of Representatives; then it is passed on by the Secretary of the Interior. In due time, he refers the matter to the National Park Service, which examines the area and evaluates its qualifications. This evaluation and that of the Secretary of the Interior are transmitted to Congress, which is then in a position to adopt the necessary resolution after giving hearings to private and public interests that may be affected by its decision.

The National Parks Association hopes that both Congress and the branches of the Executive will keep the following considerations in mind with regard to this procedure:

1.   The costs involved in the exploration of a zone proposed as a national park and in the determination of its precise qualities should be borne by the Federal government, not by the locality or region eventually to be benefited.

2.   The area and boundaries of each park should be surveyed by the National Park Service and fixed clearly by the organic law; the areas necessary to round out a preserve must be acquired at the expense of the Federal government.

3.   A report by the National Park Service, the bureau competent in such matters, is essential in deciding upon the creation of a park or upon increasing its area and including within it the essentials for preserving its fauna.

4.   The Service must have at its disposition the means for combatting fires and vandalism and for preserving the parks in the condition demanded by their importance and by the esteem in which the country holds them.

5.   Each park is to be kept intact, and there is to be no modification of its structure or characteristics unless such change is proposed jointly, after proper investigation, by the Secretary of the Interior and the Director of the National Park Service.

*   *   *

The aims that inspire these recommendations could not be clearer. Neither they nor the policies and declarations set forth earlier have been incorporated wholly into law. But their high intentions have inspired the policy that successive administrations have followed with regard to the parks and monuments. Thanks to that fact, these preserves are looked upon today as a national treasure, admirably organized and administered—areas of which every cultivated citizen of the United States may justly be proud.

Organization
of the Preserves

NATIONAL PARKS OF THE UNITED STATES

THE THIRTY national parks are: Acadia, Big Bend, Bryce Canyon, Carlsbad Caverns, Crater Lake, Everglades, Glacier, Grand Canyon, Grand Teton, Great Smoky Mountains, Haleakala National Park (Maui), Hawaii National Park (Hawaii), Hot Springs, Isle Royale, Kings Canyon, Lassen Volcanic, Mammoth Cave, Mesa Verde, Mount McKinley, Mount Rainier, Olympic, Platt, Rocky Mountains, Sequoia, Shenandoah, Virgin Islands, Wind Cave, Yellowstone, Yosemite, and Zion.

In addition to all the national parks, I have also visited several national monuments, some of which resemble the parks up to a point; and a number of historic monuments.

The following paragraphs reflect personal impressions gathered during these visits.

ORGANIZATION

The United States contains no monumental cities of architecture along classic lines, nor does it possess art treasures, properly speaking, linked to earlier epochs. But its national parks amaze all who know them. To be admired in them are marvels of nature and the prodigious work carried out by man at the service of high ideals. Nothing in the entire country is more nearly perfect in organization than the national parks.

ROAD SIGNS

Clear, succinct markers similar to the road signs along most United States highways guide visitors to the neighborhood of the particular preserve they wish to visit, no matter what route they may have chosen for their approach. Finally, a distinctive and clearly visible sign will lead to the park itself over a specially constructed road as wide and well paved as most of the roads by which they will have come. Some of the approach roads, indeed, are better: the accesses to Yellowstone and Grand Canyon would grace the entrance to a large capital. Soon the traveler sees the marker announcing that he is reaching the gate to the park. From that point on, the signs are distinguished by their rustic appearance, a rural look that does not sacrifice legibility. Whoever designed them did not forget to make them agreeable to the eye. Crude but attractive, they are made of wood—as are most of the buildings in the parks—and painted in a woody color, the paint and varnish serving only to protect them from the sun and inclement weather.

Airboats are an ideal means of transportation over the shallow waters that abound in Everglades National Park.

ROADS IN THE PARKS

The roads within the parks merit comment. Built with a view to the density and character of the traffic that uses them, at times—as in Grand Canyon, Yosemite, and Mount Rainier—they are wider than many national highways and adequate to the phenomenal traffic that flows over them in certain seasons of the year, to the size of large buses, to the extraordinary number of automobiles circulating in daylight hours, and, especially, to the need for maximum safety. Inside the parks, speed limits are reduced, and are lowered even more at dangerous spots, under the surveillance of rangers empowered to enforce the regulations.

With few exceptions, these roads are well maintained, and they have been designed with smooth grades and well-planned curves to make gear-shifting unnecessary even on the steepest slopes. As the driver raises his foot from the accelerator to reduce the speed of his car, he observes with astonishment that he is rapidly gaining altitude. No mistake is possible: every 500 or 1,000 feet the altitude is indicated on a post at the side of the road. Without noticing the climb, the driver reaches 4,500 feet . . . 6,000 . . . 7,500. At one place in Rocky Mountain National Park he will reach 12,450 feet without having slowed down. I remember one road that was narrow and dusty, surely because it was not finished when I traveled over it. But as this road is in Olympic National Park and leads to Hurricane Ridge through forests of the impressive trees native to the Pacific Coast—some of them more than one hundred feet high, straight as flagpoles, and eight feet or more through at their bases —the relative discomforts of the route were more than compensated for by the splendor of the vistas, the views of superb peaks, snow-covered even in midsummer, the solitude and remoteness of the teeth of the range, there where the storms that give Hurricane Ridge its name rage furiously in winter.

FACILITIES FOR THE VISITOR

But let us return to the markers that orient us along our way. They reflect a whole theory of good road-marking developed with the purpose of not omitting a needed sign or installing an excessive one. Such, at least, is my impression after having traveled thousands of miles through the national parks. Pertinent information can be read clearly, almost without lifting one's eyes. The signs are painted in yellow, that most easily visible of colors. The lettering is carefully done and is renewed often enough to be always legible and clear.

Thus we learn, without risk of confusion, of the location of areas reserved for camping—which are ample and well supplied with drinking water and sanitary installations—of the imminence of hotels or wooden shelters, both completely adequate for their purposes, or of restaurants, canteens, and cafeterias; of shops in which it is possible to purchase everything imaginable, from clothing appropriate to the location—light or heavy, waterproofed or not—to foodstuffs and supplies in the unending variety available elsewhere in the United States; and also souvenirs and curios of every sort; excellent postcards in color and an infinity of objects made domestically or in Japan—which, in spite of a recent war, has managed to cross frontiers and sell its products at low prices.

We see a sign indicating a narrower road—but wide enough for automobiles—leading to the residence of the superintendent of the park, or to the living quarters of the rangers, which are not so sumptuous as the former, but nevertheless are attractive. We see the way to the park museum, an important center in which we find—besides free leaflets (more than 60 million are distributed annually)—books for sale; well-selected libraries; old and modern maps; scale models; complete collections of the local wild flowers, dried or alive, some with roots exposed to facilitate study by botany enthusiasts; dis-

24

sected examples of the local fauna; historic documents; maps of the trails, which sometimes extend over hundreds of miles; sections of trunks of the largest trees—a kind of display in which the little Museum of Muir Woods National Monument, near San Francisco, is outstanding—fossils; models of geologic formations; dioramas that are always instructive and sometimes marvelous; explanations and histories of the eruptions of nearby volcanos, such as the one that formed the truncated cone at the summit of Mount Rainier, 14,408 feet above sea level, or of the glaciers and their vicissitudes through time; climatological statistics; anthropological data on the primitive inhabitants of the region—as, very notably, at Mesa Verde.

These museums come to be universities in miniature. On summer days they are crowded with visitors who scrutinize everything, with students taking notes, and children and adults pointing out to one another what they consider most important or most interesting —eager to know, gratefully taking advantage of what others wiser than they have put within their reach so that they may learn to understand, admire, and respect it.

SOMETHING ABOUT THE FAUNA

Another sign advises: "Do not feed the bears." Bears are wild animals, and dangerous. But it happens that, though wild some of the time, most of the time they are irresistible. For that reason, though violators of the no-feeding rule are liable to high fines, few refrain from feeding the bears. The ursine population of the United States today, according to recent calculations, totals 130,000 individuals divided between the only two species that exist in the country; the black bear (*ursus americanus*) and the brown or grizzly bear (*ursus horribilis*).

Both live in complete freedom in these parks, where they enjoy absolute protection. They present an incomparable and frequent spectacle, though black bears are far more numerous. I have seen dozens of them—once I saw seven together—in the national parks. Generally they wait along the roads for automobiles whose occupants will break the rules and present them with dainties, which are bolted down without squeamishness. Few things in the animal kingdom are more attractive than a female bear with her young, begging something to eat, apparently more for her offspring than for herself. I have seen sixty bears in a single week, both the larger brown ones and the smaller black ones—and that in only four parks, chiefly in Yellowstone. Some people say that sixty is the total number of bears now surviving in certain European countries where they once abounded. I hope that the time will come when we shall be able to see them again on other continents—magnificent, greedy, and inoffensive—relatively—as we can see them today in the national parks of the United States, where watching them is a delight.

All the animals in these superb parks are zealously protected by law, by the rangers, and by the public—which, by discipline and instinct, refrains from molesting them in any way. The only wild animals at times confined in enclosures are the bison (called buffalo in the United States). Although they once existed in the millions, they were almost exterminated in the nineteenth century by hunters more eager for hides than for meat. Buffalo Bill, it is said, killed 4,200 of them in a single summer. Now they are carefully protected so as to prevent their extinction. I have seen in wild state in United States and Canadian parks many moose (*alces americana*), one of them a truly magnificent specimen; many elk or, as I would rather call them, wapiti (*cervus canadensis*), including a group of three superb males, surprised early one morning; a number of pronghorns (*antilocapra americana*); several species of deer, including the

The beauty of Glacier National Park unfolds slowly and presents a different aspect at every turning of its winding roads.

mule deer (*odocoileus hemionus*) and the whitetail (*odocoileus virginianus*). I have also seen many large bighorn sheep (*ovis canadensis*) and several groups of mountain goat (*oreamnos americanus*) with white fur and short horns. I also had the luck to spot two coyotes and a wolf. The sight of these animals enjoying complete liberty is one of the most enchanting that nature offers.

During my trips through the parks, I saw many other smaller, but often supremely attractive, animals: marmots, martens, raccoons, ferrets, ground squirrels of several kinds, chipmunks, also of various kinds, and gophers, all of them rodents indigenous to the United States and Canada, in which they abound. One of the most interesting, for its pretty striped skin and its audacious, gregarious nature, is the diminutive chipmunk, an animal capable of entertaining the most blasé with the performance it will put on to be offered a nut—which, after countless hesitations and dartings forward and back, it will accept with great suavity from a human hand.

LOOKOUTS AND TRAILS

So that visitors may enjoy the panoramas that unfold from various points, the National Park Service has built many large, protected stopping places with parking facilities for automobiles. As the traveler approaches one of these lookouts, he will see a sign reading "View Point Ahead," a warning that if he wants to stop to admire the view, he should slow down. He will be able to enjoy the sight under the best conditions. From the parking areas, paths often lead to isolated points, to a nearby elevation from which the whole landscape is visible, or to little balconies, some of them built out over empty space.

In these stopping places, discreet signs point out the location of sanitary facilities for men and for women. The profusion with which these have been installed in the parks—where it is not conceived that anyone would fail to use them when they are needed—is also worthy of note, as is the almost urban profusion, and even esthetic care, with which drinking fountains have been located, generally on bases of rough stone set in cement. They are topped with chromed spigots from which crystalline drinking water emerges when one presses a button. One can easily drink directly from these fountains or fill a thermos bottle or other container—exactly as though one were in a well-furnished office or a gasoline station, with the difference that there are no bottles or paper cups in the parks.

WILD FLOWERS

Wild flowers are among the most potent enchantments of the national parks. To be present when they are at their best is an intense delight. Because they flourish most profusely in the sub-alpine fields, the best months for seeing them are July and August. Spring does not bring sufficient warmth to make them blossom; in the autumn they disappear rapidly, the latest being those which grow at lower altitudes wherever the massive, grasping trees leave them a little room.

The "wet" parks, such as Glacier, Olympic, Mount Rainier, and Yellowstone, are more hospitable to flowers, naturally, than such "dry" parks as Zion, Bryce, and Grand Canyon. Perhaps the most privileged park in this respect is Mount Rainier, where dogwood, Pacific trillium, calypso, saxifrage, phlox, Alaska spiraea, polemonium, both red and white furze, Lyall lupine, mimulus, and many others blanket the meadows with their indescribable colorings, equaling in softer tones those reached during the Spanish spring by the wild flowers of Andalusia, Extremadura, and La Mancha—not to mention the broom and viburnum that at the same season yellow the Castilian slopes.

To the natural exuberance of the national parks man has responded by dictating simple regulations that assure conservation of their flora—or by following these regulations if that is his role. No show of force or authority is required: only a request expressed simply and convincingly, the most efficient method thus far discovered for maintaining order in the parks. A notice, nothing more: "Do not cut the flowers, which delight everyone; like yourself, thousands and thousands of people [at times they could say 'hundreds of thousands'] visit this Park during the blossoming season; if each visitor picked a flower, they would soon disappear." Easy to understand—and convincing.

INTERPRETATIVE SERVICES

Mention was made earlier of the interpretative work entrusted to the National Park Service. My readers will have inferred that the purpose of this work is to clarify things that may seem obscure to the laity, developing among the visitors, without pedantry, a better understanding of the natural aspects of the parks. In carrying out this task, the Service simplifies and efficiently performs one of its inestimably valuable and eminently cultural missions. For the greatest favor that the government of the United States did its people by creating the national parks was specifically cultural.

The rest pales in comparison with this. In the parks one can breathe fresh air, one can walk, drive, admire nature, fish for trout, enjoy a relaxing vacation. But other places also offer a chance to indulge in these activities. What cannot be had elsewhere in so brief a time or so fully is education such as the national parks offer. It places the proper value upon nature and teaches men to respect and love it. And when one sees the giant advances that so-called "progress" and "civilization" have made with detriment to natural beauties—even in a territory as vast as the United States—and with grave danger to the survival of incomparable landscapes; when one remembers the disappearance, or at least the partial destruction, of splendid forests, the irruption of horrifying or merely vulgar buildings in enchanting spots; and when one thinks how we have decimated, or are able to decimate, animal species worthy of conservation and development—the bison, for example—what is being accomplished in the national parks of the United States and Canada takes on its true value as a gigantic enterprise worthy of emulation all over the world.

TALKS IN THE PARKS

Nature as a theme is immeasurable and inexhaustible. Men have devoted their whole lives to it, only to realize that they had scarcely made a beginning. The National Park Service is aware that what has been accomplished is insufficient; whole zones of inquiry remain to be explored and interpreted. But the results thus far encourage these men to persist. The more practical their labor, the more fruitful it becomes. Disquisitions on pure theory have no place here. Talks are preferred—talks given at stops during a walk, or before objects of particular interest, to groups of not more than fifty persons. At night, talks are given indoors and illustrated with colored slides or films. A twilight talk around a campfire often turns into a debate, with questions and answers on things seen during the day: mountains, geologic formations, glaciers, rocks, aquatic features, flora and fauna.

Those in charge of these talks are professors, students, or informed enthusiasts who temporarily don rangers' uniforms and dedicate their summers to this work—a custom widespread among students, who like to do some sort of summer work as a change or for self-improvement and also to defray part of the cost of their winter studies. These summer jobs are of every imaginable sort, one of them being this work in the parks.

WEEKLY PROGRAMS

Park programs are organized by the week and announced well in advance. Each day there are excursions on foot or on horseback, some long and some brief, directed by naturalists, botanists, zoologists, or geologists. Sometimes an expedition will be led by a trained photographer, who helps members of his group take the best possible pictures. The hour at which each excursion will set out is announced and adhered to; prospective members are told whether or not to bring food and advised about what to wear. Some trips are for young people; others exclude anyone under fifteen years of age unless accompanied by an adult. When the weather is unfavorable or less than six people turn up at the announced departure time, the excursions are canceled. In some of the museums, recorded talks on the objects displayed are given through a public-address system.

HELPFUL INFORMATION

I have already referred to the park trails for hikers and horseback riders. It seems almost unnecessary to say that they are marked with enough care to ensure that no possibility exists of missing the trail or getting lost. Wherever such information is desirable, signs indicate exactly where the traveler is, and the name of that mountain, this river, or that glacier. Also, the lookouts built at the edges of the roads often have orientation tables giving the names of the peaks in view and their elevation above sea level, as well as plans and printed leaflets kept under glass—which, in turn, is protected from the elements by a brass cover that the visitor closes after consulting the material.

Some national parks—Glacier and Mount Rainier among them—provide mimeographed or printed folders that the visitor finds as he wanders along a given trail. The first such folders are free; to acquire the second, the visitors must deposit a small fee in a cash-box. If they merely want to read a folder during a stop, they do so and then put it back. "All along this path," a leaflet in Mount Rainier says, "you will find numbered signs; this leaflet explains briefly the object indicated by each sign." Sometimes the object is a flower, sometimes a bush, tree, or plant. For greater clarity, some of the leaflets contain pictures of the objects described; when the plants bear fruit, the visitor is told whether or not it is edible. Thus the "What is it?" that so often escapes our lips before the mysteries of nature—relative mysteries, resulting from our ignorance—is quickly answered. A short hike, besides being delightful, can be edifying and instructive.

Some of the principal features of the larger parks—the glaciers, for example—are described in interesting mimeographed or printed literature distributed to students and others who evince interest. In the museum of each park works written about it are for sale, their prices clearly marked. Many of these are admirably edited and illustrated. Some works of this nature can also be bought in the shops that sell food, souvenirs, and gifts. Thus, for example, anyone wanting to understand the relations among common rocks or the continuous process of rock development will find what he seeks in a mimeographed leaflet. In it, a graph resembling a genealogical table will show that igneous rocks, such as granites and basalts, have evolved from others in the interior of the earth. The relation of limestone, sand, and gravel to slate, sandstone, and the conglomerates, or that between limestone and marble, will also be given.

And the reader will learn how cementing and pressure cause the first rock transformations and how heat and pressure produce marble. But if he wishes to delve deeply into geology or to increase his knowledge of botany, zoology, or glaciers, he will acquire basic works on his particular subject. He can also confine himself to buying superb colored photographs of the landscapes that lie about him in the parks.

The aims of the Information Section of the National Park Service are: (1) to develop public understanding of an area through adequate information services; (2) to foster appreciation of the totality of its values as a result of understanding; and (3) to encourage public protection of the park as a result of true understanding of its worth. In reality this is a public-relations service developed for the benefit of nature, which remains mute despite the eloquence with which it appeals to our senses and to our hearts.

THE TRAILS

To appreciate the parks fully—excellent though the roads which crisscross them are—one must take to the trails on foot or on horseback, cross alpine meadows beside placid lakes and cascades that so often attract the eye, and reach primeval zones, preserved intact. All the parks contain well-marked trails set up and maintained with care. Some of them extend for hundreds of miles and are provided with conveniently spaced-out shelters. It is easy to determine the length of a trail, the time required to cover it, and the precautions to be observed along the way.

Along the trails, warnings appear, some of them very opportune: "Riders and walkers never should leave the trails marked out for their comfort; anyone who disregards this advice runs the risk of getting lost, producing rockslides, or becoming bogged down. It is best to start out early and return to the point of departure or reach the stopping-place for the night before dark. Those who set out for isolated places must advise the chief ranger in advance. The volume of water flowing from a glacier increases enormously on warm days; for that reason, streams fordable without risk during the morning may, before twilight, become raging torrents impossible to cross. A marvelous view loses a large part of its charm if the best points from which to see it are littered with cans, papers, and other rubbish; use the receptacles installed for the disposal of garbage." The receptacles are there, you may be sure. Some of them are embedded in the ground and have lids that can be raised by means of foot-pedals—this to prevent bears from tipping them over so as to get at the remnants of food they contain.

ADVICE TO MOUNTAIN CLIMBERS

In many of the parks, it is possible to make mountain excursions or climb peaks of varying elevation and difficulty. But one must previously acquaint oneself with suitable information about the amount of time needed to reach given points, the best hour for departure in order to reach a refuge, the most adequate clothing and equipment one should wear or carry, and the need for additional advice, training, or experience. Everything has been foreseen and studied to allow the largest number of people to take advantage, under safe conditions, of everything the parks offer. Some of the instructions merit quotation:

"1. It is required that everyone register before undertaking an excursion and sign in on returning from it or reaching his destination. 2. Hikes may be undertaken only if they are carefully planned. 3. Never hike alone. 4. Take along food, water, a whistle, a compass, an electric flashlight, and flares for attracting the attention of the airplanes that may set out in search of anyone who gets lost. 5. Park automobiles where they can be seen from the air, leaving in the car a written note indicating the route you plan to take and the hour calculated for your return. 6. In case you do get lost, follow the descending course of a stream, thus not exposing yourself to the risk of circling indefinitely about the same point. 7. Three blasts on a whistle, three columns of smoke, or three flashes of an electric flashlight are the established ways of calling for help. 8. Never exhaust your physical resources; always maintain the reserve necessary to assure your personal safety."

COMPLETE PROHIBITION OF HUNTING

Hunting is absolutely forbidden in the national parks. This prohibition is rigorously enforced in keeping with one of the chief reasons for the creation of the parks: defense of the fauna that inhabit them. Nobody carries firearms or fires a shot in a park, or uses any other means for destroying or capturing animals there except on the rare occasions when, for special and sufficient reasons, the rangers are obliged to do so. In Yellowstone Park I saw a ranger capturing a bear—I don't know whether it was sick or dangerous. I stopped to watch how he was doing it—he was attracting the bear with food so as to shut it up in a sort of metal cage—but continued on my way when the ranger indicated by a wave of his hand that I should move along.

The parks contribute to the abundance of birds and animals in the regions surrounding them. They protect hunted animals, which in turn, as the preserves are not fenced in, wander freely to areas in which hunting is permitted under prescribed rules and regulations.

Though the Grand Canyon is vast and imposing when seen from the many outlooks that dot its northern and southern rims, it takes on a softer aspect if viewed from the trail that leads to the Colorado River at the foot of Grand Canyon National Park.

FISHING

On the other hand, angling for trout is permitted with rod and legal bait, but only if practiced in accordance with the rules. A special license is required for fishing in the parks, each of which makes its own regulations. Nocturnal fishing is prohibited, and the individual daily catch is limited, for example, to ten pounds of fish weighed with heads and tails, plus one additional fish, the total daily take not to exceed five fish. In some streams or sections of streams only fly-fishing is allowed.

The number of sport fishermen in the United States is incredible: the 72 million automobiles in the country have increased it greatly. In the national parks fishermen find some of the best locales for their sport; many visit the parks specifically for it. Rivers like the Gibbon and the Firehole, which join the Yellowstone to form the Madison, rank among the best trout streams in the world; others of high quality abound in other parks; at times the catches are prodigious. A spirit of sharp competition moves those who try to pre-empt the best spots along these banks, and many of them see dawn from a riverbank or lake shore as they await the supreme moment.

Instants later, the male or female, adult or child enthusiasts, with their specialized impedimenta—flies in their hats, rubber boots up to their groins or their chests—will be casting hopefully. If a lake allows fishing from boats, the needed equipment will be at hand; it could not be lacking in the United States wherever there are sufficient water to float a craft and tying-up places for launches and canoes, of which some seven and a half million are available in the country. Countless, too, are the travelers who carry a boat on top of their automobile as they set out for a summer excursion. The quiet outboard motor has proliferated extraordinarily, resulting in the development of trolling, also permitted in many lakes in the larger national parks.

RENTING OF BOATS AND HORSES

In all parks where boats or horses may be used for trips and excursions, they can be rented at prices considered reasonable by United States standards.

RESTRICTIONS ON THE INTRODUCTION OF DOMESTIC ANIMALS INTO THE PARKS

Dogs and cats may be taken into national parks only if their owners keep them leashed or in cages; for reasons easy to understand, they are not allowed otherwise. This prohibition is enforced strictly.

ADVICE FOR PHOTOGRAPHERS

The Eastman Kodak Company has published very practical illustrated folders with instructions for people using its own or other products to take color photographs in such parks as Bryce and Grand Canyon. These succinct instructions have led to the printing of astronomical quantities of pictures that, by their quality, have in turn made the attractions of the preserves widely known, bringing thousands of new visitors to them each year.

RELIGIOUS SERVICES

In the parks or their immediate surroundings there are churches and chapels of various denominations. Information about services may be obtained at ranger stations and at stopping places. Signs along the roads announce the hours of weekday Masses in Catholic churches. I remember a small chapel called the Transfiguration in one of the most isolated and beautiful areas of Grand Teton

National Park. It is built in the shape of a wooden cabin, with portico and atrium, and is consecrated for Catholic services, but its doors are open to all. And many who pass through this park visit it.

ACCOMMODATIONS IN THE PARKS AND THEIR ENVIRONS

Accommodations for travelers in the national parks are constructed, maintained, and administered by private individuals. The government lends certain facilities and grants the necessary authorizations, but does not take a direct hand in this important industry.

The mutations undergone by the tourist-accommodation industry through the years of its existence in the national parks are worth noting; here they can only be summarized briefly. From the primitive rural shack to the sumptuous large hotel was a quick step. The next move has been to apparently rough living quarters, usually isolated shelters or cabins, but endowed with all the imaginable comforts—excellent social halls, dining rooms, swimming pools, etc., grouped in central buildings to which occupants of the cabins may go whenever they wish.

In Yellowstone Park there are four large hotels, some of them now outmoded, with, respectively, 353, 311, 233, and 342 rooms and a smaller number of baths. In Grand Canyon National Park, one hotel has 256 rooms; two others have, respectively, 98 and 81 rooms. The last-mentioned hotel, magnificently located, bears the Spanish name El Tovar, to the origin of which I shall allude later on. The age of the hotels explains the fact that sometimes fewer baths than rooms, single or double, are available for guests. More rural in character is the Awahnee Hotel in Yosemite Park, with 110 rooms and well-located bathrooms. There is an attractive hotel in Glacier Park and another in Waterton Lakes National Park, Canada. Similar hotels exist in most national parks; I have mentioned only some outstanding examples.

Accommodations in the Parks and Their Environs

In their era, these hotels were considered de luxe. Some of them are still in that category, but their principal features and the tastes of their clients have changed greatly. Today people are lured by the charms of nature and want to live in intimate contact with them, and this implies isolation and a certain rusticity—the first genuine, the second more apparent than real.

What they really seek is a rough rural atmosphere endowed with every imaginable comfort: individually regulated heat in winter or on cool summer days; air-conditioning; ice-producing refrigerators; telephone; television, or at least radio; kitchen or kitchenette facilities, preferably electric, with good pantries, good lighting, and good utensils and dishes. A wood-burning fireplace with dry wood piled alongside is a cosy adjunct on cool forest evenings. And through the large windows it is pleasant to watch, after daybreak or in the late afternoon, soft landscapes or imposing panoramas, and large bears—which pretend to roam about, but in reality come in search of a mouthful—or deer and stags with their agile fawns. This combination of comfort and attractiveness in a cabin of rude exterior, is the ideal—and I do not even mention the luxurious chairs, the beds, the perfect bathroom fixtures, with hot and cold water at all times, or the attractive appearance of the rooms. All this is taken for granted. It is a pleasure to live in a national park; Adam and Eve had to make do with less, but even so considered their habitation a paradise.

Hotels with 400 and more rooms no longer are erected in national parks and their environs, and the new accommodations demonstrate that there was a need for this change. Let us glance briefly at what is being done now to house the seventy-eight million or so visitors who go to the national parks each year:

(a) *Tents for Camping.* For the campers, who are legion, a tent suffices. They carry it with them to the parks, install it and its indispensable paraphernalia, and dismantle it when their vacation is over. The Park Service designates and takes care of the camping sites, supplying them with wood and drinking water. The campers buy their food at central points and cook it to their own tastes in kitchens placed within easy reach. Camping areas have sanitary installations, use of which is obligatory, as well as washbowls and showers. In some parks, private concessionaires rent, among other things, beds, mattresses, small cooking and heating apparatus, lanterns, blankets, tables, and chairs; there are also permanent open-air tables surrounded by benches. Only dead wood may be used for burning, and campers are required to keep the sites clean, to burn any combustible rubbish with every precaution, and to throw any unburnable rubbish into the receptacles provided. The first camper to arrive has first choice of location. A word to the wise: edibles should be kept in boxes and hung high in the trees, as bears are given to devouring anything edible left within their reach in automobiles or camping sites.

(b) *Isolated Cabins.* In some of the parks it is common to see isolated cabins spread out through woods or grouped beside a lake or river. These contain the minimum comforts needed for modest living during a few days or a fortnight. They are often used by older people who find camping out a little too arduous.

(c) *Motels.* Located near the parks—but never in them—motels are preferred by many travelers. Were they not available, fewer people would visit these marvels. The motels serve as bases from which the parks can be visited. People stopping in them go to cafeterias for midday meals, to the nearest restaurants for breakfast and dinner.

(d) *De Luxe Cabins.* Constructed by the most advanced techniques, handsomely decorated and furnished, grouped around a central building containing all the social rooms, these are the pre-

In Grand Teton National Park, Mount Teewinot raises its head over still waters and forested slopes.

ferred accommodations of visitors who wish to live comfortably in close contact with nature.

"HELP US TO PROTECT THIS PARK"

This plea comes to us, almost anxiously, from the pages of the descriptive folders published by the National Park Service. In addition to explaining the purposes of the parks, the folders ask visitors to co-operate with the Service in preserving them, giving a lesson in civics which few people disregard—though cases of negligence do occur. With special emphasis they ask the public not to touch or disfigure the trees, plants, and other vegetation, the rocks, minerals, buildings, and signs; to take nothing out of the park without the written permission of its superintendent; not to feed, irritate, or molest the animals and birds.

If a fire must be lighted outside the places designated as camp-sites, special authorization must be obtained, as it must for launching or using one's own boat. Instructions to drivers of automobiles are very precise. They are admitted to some of the parks on payment of one dollar per automobile for a circulation pass good for fifteen days or of two dollars for an annual one. These modest fees provide one of the principal sources of the Service's income.

THE PARKS SEEN FROM THE AIR

Airplane flights are prohibited in some parks because forest fires could result from the crash of a plane with its tanks full of gasoline. In Grand Canyon National Park, where this risk is small because trees are scarce, flights are allowed. The exception is a notable one: the best way to see the Grand Canyon of the Colorado is to fly over it, some 1,000 feet above its rims, with the great river in view and the colors of its cliffs glowing in the sun.

44

Small, slow planes make these flights, taking off from a nearby field. The charge is moderate: $15 for two people for a forty-minute flight, $30 for three passengers for a longer flight. If a passenger is a photographer as well, the pilot will assist him by making all the turns and dips compatible with safety so that he may get the best shots.

WHAT TO DO IN EACH PARK

Descriptive folders tell the visitor to a given park how best to use the time at his disposition. The Park Service knows that from this sort of help the public derives one of its major satisfactions, the parks themselves some of their most effective propaganda.

THE DANGER OF FIRE

Fire is the greatest menace that park personnel must ward against and fight. The consequences of fire may be disastrous, as we can see, for example, in Acadia, the delightful Maine park, or in Rocky Mountain National Park, in Colorado. In the latter park especially, we still see traces of three or four huge nineteenth-century conflagrations that devastated immense forests, which have not yet recovered fully.

The struggle against fire is well organized, and the Service and its rangers do everything they can. But the danger is great, above all in the parks located in the central and southern United States, where, despite the leafiness and verdancy of the woods, the air is dry and temperatures soar in summer. Exhortations to the public are incessant. On all sides there are warnings and pleas: "Lighting fires is permitted only in the areas reserved as campsites, never near the roots of trees, dry wood or leaves, moss or vegetable residues. Once a fire is lighted under the proper conditions, never leave it;

before departing, you must put it out with water. Do not trust to luck; make certain that the fire you lighted is completely extinguished. It is absolutely prohibited to throw cigars, cigarettes, and matches, even though no longer burning, on highways and trails. Deposit these remains in the ashtray in your car or, if you are on foot, reduce them to dust with the sole of your shoe. Only by special permission may a fire be lighted in the open air outside the areas indicated for camping."

Fires occur in the national parks, nevertheless, though fortunately they are rare. Would fewer fires have broken out in these areas if the parks had not been established—if, precisely because they had not been established, these areas had received fewer visitors? Decidedly no, categorically no. Such are the precautions taken, aside from the advice and warnings sampled above; such are the firebreaks, observation posts, and other means for fighting blazes, the civic education of the visitors, and their disposition to co-operate with the authorities in preventing and combating fire, that the question can be answered flatly. The risk of destructive fires would be much greater if no national parks existed in these incomparable wooded areas abounding in fallen leaves and wood.

3

Description of the National Parks

T HE EXISTENCE of thirty large national parks within the territory of one nation implies a possibility of a certain sameness among them, a risk of monotony, resulting from the repetition of themes. But even if for the moment we leave out Alaska, Hawaii, Puerto Rico, and the Virgin Islands, the United States is more a continent than a country; the differences between its well-defined regions are remarkable. The National Park Service has seen to it that each park "differs from the rest, so that the totality of the System represents the greatest possible variety of typical zones, all of them of supreme quality." This was one of the most praiseworthy purposes behind the creation of these preserves.

In fact, the parks differ widely. I have visited them all; there is no doubt that the above-mentioned aim has been achieved. By rare good luck, a different natural element seems to have been assigned the star role in each park.

*   *   *

In its cragginess, the coast of Maine resembles the coast of Galicia near Finisterre. In one of its most beautiful and moving regions lies Acadia National Park. There the Atlantic, breaking incessantly on enormous rocks, outlines a forest landscape strewn with lakes and offering many vantage points for enjoying magnificent panoramas. Acadia interrupts a succession of picturesque villages along a shore much frequented in summer. Near it are such fashionable resorts as Bar Harbor and islands like Dark Harbor, the summer home of millionaires. If it were not for Acadia, surely the most "civilized" of the parks, this segment of the Maine coast would have lost its primeval flavor long ago. It retains it despite signs of a fire caused by carelessness in 1947, the scars of which still are visible; this fire destroyed some 10,000 acres of pines, silver firs, spruce, beeches, birches, red planetrees, and cedars, the most abundant trees in this forest.

*   *   *

In Big Bend National Park, Texas, one is impressed by the uninterrupted view of vast areas of multicolored terrain stretched out beneath an immense azure canopy on serene days, when the air is free of the dust that the winds often carry. We are in the south, in lands that Cabeza de Vaca was the first white man to cross as he fled from Florida in 1535, when he spent eight months journeying through swamps, deserts, and mountains to rejoin his compatriots

48

in Mexico. The transparency of the atmosphere makes it possible to see vast distances; the gray steepnesses of the Sierra del Carmen across the border seem close to Casa Grande and other peaks of the Chisos Mountains, the highest in the park, believed by the primitive inhabitants to be bewitched and to possess mysterious powers. Big Bend takes its name from the wide curve that the Rio Grande makes as it forms the boundary between Texas and the Mexican states of Chihuahua and Coahuila, gliding between the cliffs of three imposing canyons: Santa Elena, Mariscal, and Boquillas, on the other side of which it is hoped that Mexico some day will establish a park that, with Big Bend, would constitute a huge international preserve. The blue waters of the Rio Grande give the only moist tone to a landscape that is mostly desert, covered with such tropical plants as ocotillo and creosote bush, lechuguilla and yucca, and by nopal and pitaya cactus, with their delicious fruit and beautiful flowers. On the slopes of the mountains grow pinyon pine, juniper, sumach, and maguey; higher up, there are ponderosa pine, Douglas fir, Arizona cypress, quaking aspen, and strawberry trees. From the Mina Perdida trail, the horizon has no limit; the sun's rays, which in winter inundate the landscape with color, foretell the heat of summer.

*   *   *

The brush of a Monet rather than an inept pen is needed to describe Bryce Canyon. Even more than the amazing rock formations carved out by the rain, the wind, and the frost, assisted by the passage of time, what impresses one in Bryce is the color. The Paiute Indians, seeking to interpret the magic characteristics of this fairy-tale place, invented to describe them the term *Unka-timpe-wa-wince-*

49

pockick, which may be translated as "red rocks standing like men in a cup-shaped canyon." On a sunny summer day, with white clouds scudding rapidly across the intense azure of the sky and the distant ranges standing sharp against the horizon, the colors of Bryce, against the greens of the ponderosa pine and quaking aspen, display an incredible gamut of reds, roses, yellows, and blues. It is the most fantastic spectacle of its kind imaginable; I shall always have on the retina of my memory the colors that Bryce so generously lavishes.

*   *   *

Two things particularly arouse our admiration in Carlsbad Caverns: the tremendous proportions of this, the largest cave in the world, and the remarkable work that men have carried out to facilitate access to it. The Big Room of the Caverns, located in a national park covering some fifty thousand acres in the Guadalupe Mountains of New Mexico, lies about 875 feet below the point at which the descent is started, an easy descent thanks to a safe, gently sloping pathway a little less than two miles long. Near the entrance to the cave, and from just outside it, one can watch, at suitable times, the flight of millions of bats. Going down into the cave, one makes a descent comparable to that between the top and bottom floors of an 83-story building; the trip is not tiring, however, for anyone with normal physical endurance. Eight stories, or some eighty-five feet, above the Big Room—around which level paths extend for more than a mile—we enter the big dining room, in which hundreds of visitors can be served simultaneously. The washrooms situated on this level are notable for their size and installations and for the efficiency with which they are ventilated. A bank of swift, roomy elevators communicates with the exterior. The tours, often made up of more than eight hundred people at one time, are admirably conducted. Everything has been foreseen to facilitate contemplation of the marvels that these incomparable caverns offer. The lighting is not too bright; and it does not fail. The stops along the way are intelligently planned, and during them the public is seated to listen to relevant but never pedantic explanations by the rangers, who tell us enough so that we can understand the category and importance of the sights before our eyes: the Greek Lake, the King's Palace, the Queen's Chamber, crystal lotuses among crystalline waters, forests of stalactites, columns of onyx, petrified lace, and draperies of marble.

*   *   *

What we see in Crater Lake National Park, located in southern Oregon, is the crater of an extinct volcano, almost round and half filled by the blue waters of a lake more than six miles in diameter and nearly two thousand feet deep—the depth equaling the distance from the surface of the lake to the tops of the peaks that surround it. The water appears calm, but in color and formations the rocks of the cliffs suggest a petrified tempest. A spacious highway, situated 7,500 feet and more above sea level, circles the lake, turning aside at regular intervals from the circumference toward well-constructed lookouts from which superb vistas unfold. Crater Lake is one of the few spectacles of large size in the national parks which can be absorbed all at once. What one sees is of incomparable loveliness and majesty. The blue of the water recalls that of the Mediterranean at a few privileged spots in Majorca and along the Costa Brava of Catalonia.

51

In his admirable book, *The National Parks,* published by Alfred A. Knopf in 1951, Freeman Tilden recalls that in 1853, when the lake was first discovered, it was named Deep Blue Lake. Rediscovered in 1862, it was called Blue Lake. Three years later, two soldiers christened it Lake Majesty. Finally it became Crater Lake, and Tilden is probably right in saying that this name is the best one, for what one sees is a lake in a crater. Yet what impresses one most is the color of its waters, that incomparable and mysterious blue which is equally blue when it reflects the leaden hues of dark gray clouds as when it mirrors a limpid sky.

*   *   *

The immense Everglades National Park covers 1,258,591 acres at the extreme southern tip of Florida, and is consequently of a marked tropical character. In this part of the world the landscape has two principal features: vast flat expanses of perennial green dotted with small clumps of trees and bushes which extend to infinity a few yards above the level of the water, and watery areas, with islets thickly covered with vegetation. Both provide refuge for hundreds of millions of land and sea birds: white ibis, wood ibis, seven varieties of heron, anhingas that resemble serpents when swimming, many sorts of duck, Florida and purple gallinules, various bitterns, kingfishers, white and brown pelicans, marine crows, falcons, cranes, eagles, vultures, kites, swift-striking ospreys, white-headed and black-headed coots, and, finally, American or reddish egrets and spoonbills or pink flamingos, which but for the existence of sanctuaries like the Everglades would have disappeared long since, victims of man's relentless persecution. Despite such sanctuaries, the risk of extermination persists, though now for other reasons, principally progress or so-called civilization. Alligators also abound—I counted almost sixty of them, half submerged in water a foot deep around an islet—as do black bear, nutria, puma, and fox. But the most impressive fauna of the park, the organization of which has been brought to extraordinary perfection in a short time, are the ibis, the egrets, and the roseate spoonbills, birds of incredible beauty that nest in the mangrove trees on the fragile branches of which they pose by the dozen, giving marvelous displays of equilibrium and cleverness when they unmistakably identify their own eggs and broods among the masses of both that exist in the foliage.

*　　　*　　　*

I suggest that anyone going to Glacier National Park, Montana, enter it through the little village of St. Mary, near the lake of the same name, to which some time should be allotted. If the visitor proceeds on foot or on horseback along any one of the trails that extend for more than a thousand miles through this park, he will have a better chance to appreciate the scenery, which is exceptionally beautiful. Emerging to greet him as he moves along will be male and female bears and their cubs; other representatives of the local fauna will keep their distance, neither begging for nor accepting any gift whatsoever, but reflecting in their mild and confident mien the good treatment they receive from man. Through a car window the panorama unrolls like a ribbon, at a distance that generally permits the visitor to appreciate its splendor fully. The forests are dense; their trees climb the flanks of the mountains, giving way, higher up, to humble grasses and alpine plants; these latter, too, thin out, until at a given altitude only hard stone can resist the rigors of the cold, which at last conquers it also, burying it in snow the year around. Signs of human habitation vanish. Down the sheer wall of high cliffs threads of icy water run; rivulets surge out of glaciers; fields are dampened by drops of rain or dew. Streams are born and flow together, quickly gathering torrential force. Fed by springs in the moist, broad basins, they soon become rivers. And the waters of these rivers, rushing over waterfalls, spread out on level ground to form vast lakes, tossed by the winds or left majestically serene or frozen hard in winter. Such is Glacier, the northernmost National Park outside Alaska. It abuts on almost equally beautiful Canadian areas and encloses no less than fifty glaciers, as well as two hundred lakes. These latter, like some of the glaciers, are partly visible from the daring highway, bordering high precipices and dominating spectacular vistas along some fifty miles, which preserves the name that the Indians gave to a nearby peak: Going-to-the-Sun. At Logan Pass it crosses the Continental Divide, from which the waters run down in four distinct directions: toward the Pacific Ocean through the Fraser and Columbia river basins; toward the Atlantic through the Saint Lawrence River; toward icy Hudson's Bay; and toward the Gulf of Mexico, nineteen hundred miles away.

*   *   *

Sunlight is the master of ceremonies that calls upon the colors in the Grand Canyon of the Colorado River, the pride of Arizona and internationally famous. Without the sun, the clefts and crevices of this park would not gleam as resplendently as they do on a clear day at morning or at sundown, when the sun's rays, filtering through fissures in the rocks, best display their forms and colors, filling the landscape with imponderable grandeur and magnificence, creating the cathedrals, soaring towers, and palaces, ephemeral fantasies that irrupt from the shadows in which a passing cloud has wrapped them and then sink back into mystery after dazzling the onlooker with their glory. Each hour, almost each minute, varies the spectacle without diminishing its grandeur—the grandeur of a canyon unique in the world, more than 210 miles in length, with a maximum depth of more than one mile, a width of between three and a half and eighteen miles. The aridity of its walls is relieved by the humid contrast of the broad waters of the Colorado—one of the largest rivers of North America, which runs more than two thousand miles from its source to the Gulf of California—as well as by the greenness of the trees of the splendid Kaibab National Forest lying to the south and north of this prodigious defile.

*   *   *

Grand Teton National Park, Wyoming, is not far from Yellowstone: that so many beauties and so many things of interest should be found so close together is in itself remarkable. Grand Teton is much smaller than Yellowstone: 299,580 acres as against 2,213,207, a circumstance that increases its popularity with many people who prefer less vast dimensions and more intimate attractions. The charms of Grand Teton unfold in full magnificence to those who travel down its valley from north to south. On the opposite shore of big Jackson Lake the Tetons rise from the water's edge, soaring to a great height—the highest of the peaks tops 13,750 feet, its silhouette recalling the Yordas in Spain as one gazes at it among its companions from the best vantage point, alongside the highway from Riaño to the Puerto del Pontón, where a fine *parador* now is located.

55

Great Smoky Mountains National Park is in its full glory in spring and autumn, when its flowers and foliage burst into masses of bright or mellow color.

*   *   *

Great Smoky Mountains National Park, along with Grand Canyon, Yosemite, Rocky Mountain, and Yellowstone, is among the most visited of the national parks. It owes its extraordinary popularity not only to the magnificent landscapes that can be seen as one travels through it, but even more to its outstanding vegetation in spring and autumn. In spring, the park is famous for the blossoms of its dogwood, mountain laurel, ciclamor, azalea, and, above all, rhododendron—the dense bushes profuse with white, pink, and violet flowers that astonish and delight onlookers. Good trails facilitate visits to sites of especially noteworthy explosions of color. To admire the autumn blossoms, it is best to use the lookouts; from them stretch panoramas embellished with all the tonalities that are the park's leading attractions at this time of year. Great Smoky seems larger than it is—the highway that traverses it from north to south measures only a little more than thirty miles—thanks to the elevations reached by successive mountain masses split by narrow valleys. Several points reach altitudes of nearly 6,600 feet. As with other much-visited parks, the nearby concentration of hotels and other tourist accommodations is notable.

*   *   *

On July 1, 1961, Haleakala National Park, on the island of Maui —until then a part of Hawaii National Park—became a separate unit, the thirtieth established on United States territory. Most of it lies within a huge volcano, after which it is named. The mountain, which is thirty-three miles long and twenty-four miles wide at sea level, rises to an elevation of 10,025 feet. Its crater is seven and a half miles long and two and a half miles wide; it lies 3,000 feet below the present summit of the mountain and is twenty-one miles in circumference; the tallest of the cinder cones rises 1,000 feet from the crater floor. The area is not only impressive, but also beautiful. Several hikes, long and short, can be recommended. One unforgettable experience is the guided trip by horseback into the crater, with an overnight stay in a mountain hut; arrangements can be made at the Silversword Inn (altitude 6,800 feet), the loftiest hostelry in the islands. The Inn takes its name from a beautiful plant as famous as the crater itself and remarkable for the lustrous silvery down that thickly covers its leaves.

*   *   *

Hawaii National Park, on the island of Hawaii, lies around two active volcanoes, Kilauea and Mauna Loa. In 1952, in only half an hour, four million cubic yards of lava poured through a crack in the floor of the Halemaumau pit of Kilauea. There have been several eruptions since then, visible from the terraces and windows of Volcano House, where comfortable accommodations are available within the park. More than 2,000 square miles of the island are covered by lava flows from Mauna Loa, which rises 13,680 feet above sea level; its periods of quiet range from a few months to as long as nine years. Along the northeast rim of Kilauea Crater roads run through the upper edge of a tropical rain forest with many varieties of ferns shaded by ohia trees. Clumps of koa, soapberry, kolea, and mamane trees are also to be seen in the surrounding district. Birds as beautiful as the apapani, the amakihi, the elepaio, and the iiwi add color and life to the thickets. Pheasant and quail, wild pigs, wild goats, and mongoose live on the slopes of Mauna Loa. A visit to the City of Refuge, a national historical park established recently on the island of Hawaii, should not be missed.

*   *   *

Hot Springs is a spa of mineral-medicinal waters located in the Ouachita Mountains of Arkansas, a region of beautiful forests and big lakes which was declared a national park in order to preserve the beneficial properties of the springs, which had been known for centuries. The daily flow of these springs is some 1,200,000 gallons at a temperature of 140° Fahrenheit, produced, it is said, by igneous rocks in the subsoil which heat water that sinks down from surface precipitation and then is forced back to the surface through faults in the stratifications. Other people attribute the high temperature, perhaps with less reason, to the action of these subterranean rocks on currents of water that have not reached the surface previously. In Hot Springs the bathing establishments, like the hydrotherapeutic and related treatments, are subject to scrupulous regulation. As in many other parks, the museum in Hot Springs National Park is worth a visit.

*   *   *

For most people, Isle Royale may be the least accessible of the national parks. Located in the northwestern part of Lake Superior, the second largest lake in the world, this park is twenty miles from the Canadian shore, a like distance from that of Minnesota, and seventy miles from the shores of Wisconsin and Michigan. Long and narrow, Isle Royale measures forty-five miles from end to end;

its maximum width is only nine miles. No wheeled traffic circulates here: the island fortunately lacks roads. But on foot or on horseback one can easily travel through it by trails that lead to numerous lakes and rove among the chain of hills, the island's spine, which divides its waters. Its greatest elevation, Mount Desor, reaches an altitude of more than 1,270 feet. The island was inhabited in prehistoric times by Indians who crudely exploited its copper deposits. It is covered with thick forests of various pines, aspen, cedar, juniper, ash, and birch. In 1936 a big forest fire, traces of which will endure a century or more, leveled a large part of the forest. Isle Royale National Park is at its best during the summer months. Thirty-six varieties of orchids flourish there; wild fruits abound. Two hundred small islets mark the indented shoreline; at times the coves resemble miniature Norwegian fjords or small Galician river harbors, offering ideal conditions for motorboating and sailing and secure landing-places for seaplanes. Well run and well organized, this park soon will witness a considerable increase in the number of visitors.

*   *   *

Kings Canyon owes its name to Spaniards, who discovered it one January 6 and named the region in honor of the Three Magi: "Canyon of the Three Kings." Located in the heart of the Sierra Nevada, the great eastern California cordillera that rises to snowcapped peaks 13,000 feet and more above sea level, it makes an indescribable impression. Enormous granitic masses form domes that border the principal river of the canyon—Kings River—and are themselves dominated by exalted mountains, behind which rise the towering peaks of the Sierra. The variety of landscape is enormous. Torrents descend in impetuous cascades to waters on whose beds lie rocks and boulders brought down by heavier freshets. A daring highway, hewn out of living rock, its highest section bordered by giant sequoias, allows visitors to contemplate the panorama while driving at the edge of steep declivities for fifty miles. The waters of Kings River, of a marvelous blue-green, flow turbulent or serene according to their depth. When they reach the calm plains, they water the grass of smooth fields dotted with thick trees and covered with flowers. A few steps to the right or the left, and we find ourselves again in the forest. Beyond the trees rise the granitic cliffs of the canyon, down which other waters merrily run, eager to join those of the river.

*　　　*　　　*

Within a relatively small area of 104,212 acres, Lassen Volcanic National Park encompasses some of the most beautiful panoramas in the United States. Few preserves of its rank offer landscapes with such lively contrasts; from forests consisting chiefly of conifers of various sorts and huge size—ponderosa pines among them—to smooth lakes of peaceful waters such as Butte, Reflection, and Manzanita, which mirror the vegetation and the surrounding peaks; from visions of romantic distance to the green of the forests in the foreground, crowned by the teeth of the Cascades, which stretch across Oregon and Washington to distant Canada, and to the only volcano in the continental United States outside Alaska which has passed through periods of intense activity in recent times. The volcano's devastations, principally caused by torrents of lava and mud, destroyed whole forests, some of them more than three miles away. Still to be seen at various spots are fumaroles and springs of boiling water, which form lovely rainbows as they emerge; sulphurous emanations also are frequent. A good example of the perfect organization of the park is the extremely useful guidebook to the highway that crosses it from Manzanita to Mineral. Sketches and paragraphs of instructive reading matter aré numbered to correspond to numbers on tablets along the road. One needs only to stop at such a marker and refer to the guide to identify the peak in the distance, the specific properties of a hydrothermal area, the reason why some tree roots lie on the surface of the ground, the exact elevation of the ground on which we stand, the volcanic causes of the colorings of some rocks, the glacial origin of Emerald Lake, the spot to which a trail starting at our feet can lead us, what is needed for climbing Mount Lassen if one follows another trail off the highway, the kind of clothing and impedimenta advisable for spending an hour at an altitude of 9,800 feet, the precautions to be taken during a climb, what can be seen in the distance from a well-placed lookout, the fauna of the area, the names of the wild flowers (which visitors are requested not to touch) and of the birds that fly about.

*   *   *

The caverns of Mammoth Cave National Park, in the heart of Kentucky, lie at five distinct underground levels, some of them at a depth of 355 feet. The caves and galleries thus far explored extend for a total of 150 miles; throughout their full length, because of phenomena not yet explained, one breathes pure fresh air. A series of well-planned tours through the interior of the caverns annually allow thousands of visitors to see everything of interest in the caves, which are vestiges of the action of water at a time set by geologists at 240 million years ago. In the caverns, lakes and rivers can be traversed in boats; to be seen are stalactites, stalagmites, cascades,

Isle Royale National Park, a cluster of islands in Lake Superior only twenty miles from the shores of Canada and Minnesota, impresses the visitor with a sense of remoteness.

domes, and other petrified forms of great beauty. Existence without light for millions of years in the depths of these caverns has brought about a species of sightless fish. The park also contains handsome tree-covered areas. It extends over an area of seventy-eight square miles.

*   *   *

The forests of Mesa Verde, in Colorado, are abundant. Its panoramas are airy and open. But its chief interest, apart from its beauty, lies in prehistoric and pre-Columbian ruins that have enabled archaeologists to reconstruct much of the life and customs of the primitive inhabitants of this section of the United States. So as to make these ruins accessible to visitors—so as to "interpret" them, I should say more exactly—the National Park Service has carried out here a plan that merits the highest praise. To preserve these ruins intact, it prohibits entrance into many historic dwellings; on the other hand, it permits access to others that it cares for, maintains, and explains through talks by the rangers who accompany any groups entering the area of the ruins. For good reasons, the park museum is extraordinarily interesting and comprehensive. There, in addition to an excellent library, visitors are offered explanations that equip them to take full advantage of their trip. This procedure provides an excellent opportunity for intelligent study of a rudimentary civilization, a page from a history that passed through diverse phases and achieved its classic period in the twelfth and thirteenth centuries, followed thereafter by a tremendous drought of twenty-four years which drove the Indians who had inhabited these dwellings to abandon them completely.

Mount McKinley National Park, Alaska, established in 1917, is the second largest of the national parks: it covers more than 3,000 square miles. Swallowed up in the vast surrounding landscapes, its huge proportions nonetheless impress the visitor profoundly. They are dwarfed, however, by the impressive sight of the mountain which gives the park its name and which the Indians called Denali, "The High," long before it received its present name. It lifts its summit, the highest point of North America, to 20,300 feet, and has as neighbors such formidable peaks as Mount Foraker, Mount Silverthorne, and Mount Russell, with which it forms a cordillera of staggering majesty and grandeur. At its foot, within the confines of the park, the shapeless masses of dark gray glaciers seem to advance menacingly upon the spectator. From east to west, two thirds of the park is traversed by a magnificent highway built by the National Park Service as an access route for the many visitors. From the section that stretches between Camp Eielson and beautiful Wonder Lake, one has, on fine days, a marvelous view of Mount McKinley and the entire range. Mammals abound in this park, the principal varieties being Dall sheep, grizzly bear, caribou, and moose; there are also rodents, including marmot, as well as Canada lynx, coyote, fox, and a rabbit whose fur changes color with the seasons. Among the birds are many that can withstand the wintry rigors: the ptarmigan or striped partridge also varies the shading of its plumage to protect itself during the changing seasons. But most of the birds are migratory. Mount McKinley National Park, whose slopes become covered with splendid colors at the onset of the premature autumn, is accessible during the warmest months by the Denali Highway, linking it with the chief cities of Alaska, and at all times of the year by the Alaska Railroad, which runs from Anchorage to Fairbanks.

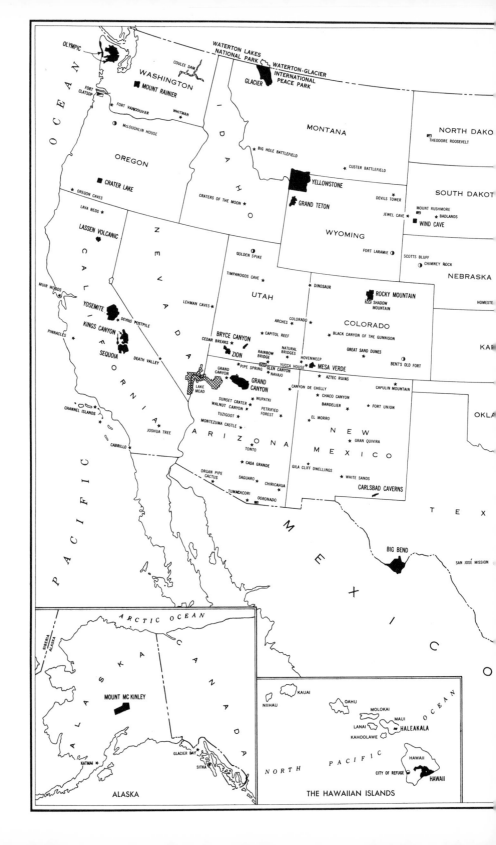

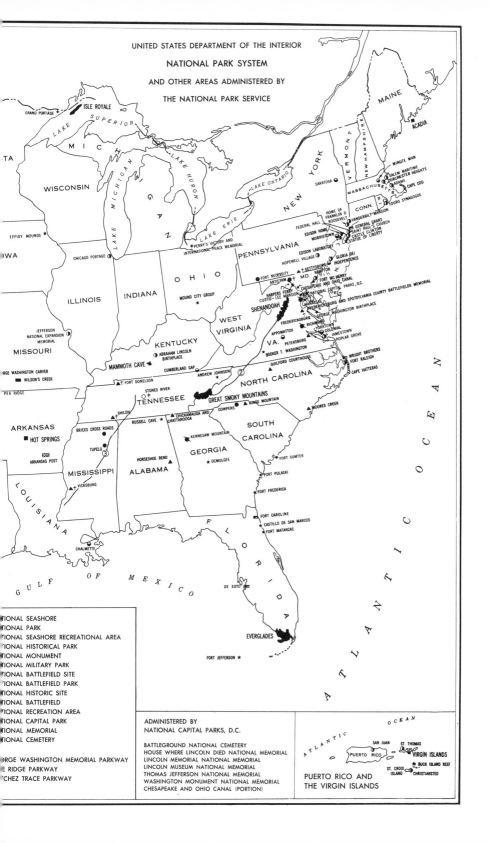

UNITED STATES DEPARTMENT OF THE INTERIOR

NATIONAL PARK SYSTEM

AND OTHER AREAS ADMINISTERED BY

THE NATIONAL PARK SERVICE

GRAND PORTAGE ▲ ISLE ROYALE

LAKE SUPERIOR

MICHIGAN

WISCONSIN

LAKE MICHIGAN

LAKE HURON

MAINE

ACADIA

MINUTE MAN

NEW YORK

VERMONT

NEW HAMPSHIRE

SALEM MARITIME
DORCHESTER HEIGHTS
ADAMS   CAPE COD
TOURO SYNAGOGUE

SARATOGA

MASSACHUSETTS

CONN.

LAKE ONTARIO

EFFIGY MOUNDS ✳

IOWA

CHICAGO PORTAGE ◐

PERRY'S VICTORY AND
INTERNATIONAL PEACE MEMORIAL

LAKE ERIE

PENNSYLVANIA

HOME OF
FRANKLIN D
ROOSEVELT

VANDERBILT MANSION

FEDERAL HALL   GENERAL GRANT
                  SAINT PAUL'S CHURCH
EDISON HOME   CASTLE CLINTON
MORRISTOWN   STATUE OF LIBERTY

EDISON LABORATORY

HOPEWELL VILLAGE ▲   GLORIA DEI
                    INDEPENDENCE

OHIO

INDIANA

ILLINOIS

MOUND CITY GROUP
        ✳

WEST
VIRGINIA

KENTUCKY

GETTYSBURG
ANTIETAM
FORT NECESSITY   MD.

HAMPTON

FORT MC HENRY
CHESAPEAKE AND OHIO CANAL
NATIONAL CAPITAL PARKS, D.C.

HARPERS FERRY
CUSTIS-LEE MANSION

SHENANDOAH   MANASSAS
                  FREDERICKSBURG AND SPOTSYLVANIA COUNTY BATTLEFIELDS MEMORIAL
            FREDERICKSBURG
            RICHMOND   GEORGE WASHINGTON BIRTHPLACE
VA.   YORKTOWN
APPOMATTOX COLONIAL
            JAMESTOWN
PETERSBURG POPLAR GROVE

JEFFERSON
NATIONAL EXPANSION
MEMORIAL

MISSOURI

ABRAHAM LINCOLN
BIRTHPLACE

MAMMOTH CAVE ◯

BOOKER T. WASHINGTON

WRIGHT BROTHERS
FORT RALEIGH

CUMBERLAND GAP

GUILFORD COURTHOUSE

CAPE HATTERAS

GEORGE WASHINGTON CARVER
    ▪ WILSON'S CREEK

ANDREW JOHNSON ②

NORTH CAROLINA

PEA RIDGE

FORT DONELSON ▲†

STONES RIVER
◯†

SHILOH

TENNESSEE   GREAT SMOKY MOUNTAINS

KINGS MOUNTAIN

CHICKAMAUGA AND
CHATTANOOGA   COWPENS

MOORES CREEK

ARKANSAS

BRICES CROSS ROADS

RUSSELL CAVE ✳

▪ HOT SPRINGS

SOUTH
CAROLINA

KENNESAW MOUNTAIN

ARKANSAS POST

TUPELO
③

HORSESHOE BEND

GEORGIA

FORT SUMTER

MISSISSIPPI   ALABAMA

✳ OCMULGEE

FORT PULASKI

VICKSBURG ▲†

LOUISIANA

FORT FREDERICA

FORT CAROLINE
CASTILLO DE SAN MARCOS
FORT MATANZAS

CHALMETTE

GULF   OF   MEXICO

DE SOTO ✳

FLORIDA

ATLANTIC OCEAN

EVERGLADES

FORT JEFFERSON ✳

ADMINISTERED BY
NATIONAL CAPITAL PARKS, D.C.

BATTLEGROUND NATIONAL CEMETERY
HOUSE WHERE LINCOLN DIED NATIONAL MEMORIAL
LINCOLN MEMORIAL NATIONAL MEMORIAL
LINCOLN MUSEUM NATIONAL MEMORIAL
THOMAS JEFFERSON NATIONAL MEMORIAL
WASHINGTON MONUMENT NATIONAL MEMORIAL
CHESAPEAKE AND OHIO CANAL (PORTION)

OCEAN

ATLANTIC

SAN JUAN   ST. THOMAS

PUERTO RICO   VIRGIN ISLANDS

ST. CROIX   BUCK ISLAND REEF
ISLAND   CHRISTIANSTED

PUERTO RICO AND
THE VIRGIN ISLANDS

An excellent hotel, named for the park, is open annually from June 8 to September 8.

*   *   *

The chief attraction in Mount Rainier National Park is the mountain itself, a tremendous truncated cone covered with snow and soaring 14,408 feet above sea level. This is a volcano of vast proportions and white slopes, whose most recent eruption apparently occurred early in the nineteenth century. Mount Rainier is the fourth highest mountain in the continental United States outside Alaska, and it is topped only a little by (in this order) Mount Whitney, Mount Elbert, and Mount Massive. There is a striking contrast between Rainier's snowy peak and the placid fields of bright colors around its base—itself at a considerable altitude but with exuberant vegetation and air of incredible transparency.

*   *   *

In Olympic National Park, discovered by Juan Pérez in 1774, the outstanding feature—despite the magnificence of Mount Olympus, which rises almost from the seashore to more than 7,800 feet, and despite the corpulent trees that soar straight toward the light—is the rain forest produced by centuries of constant moisture in the thickness of the woods and valleys that slope downward toward the Pacific. Located in the state of Washington, this park faces north over Juan de Fuca Strait, a name recalling a Spanish expedition that is said, possibly on insufficient evidence, to have sailed these waters in 1592. Across this arm of water one can clearly see Vancouver Island, British Columbia. Olympic is one of the national parks least provided with wide highways and minor roads. The accesses, at several separate points, consist almost exclusively of trails, and it is by following these into the forest that we can find the marvelous concentrations of many varieties of cedar, ash, and pine dripping moisture over a forest floor covered with smooth moss and huge ferns that grow unhurriedly, not measuring time, in a diversity of forms and shades of green and surrounded by mystery and silence.

*　　　*　　　*

Platt National Park, Oklahoma, with an area of 912 acres, is the smallest of the national parks, enclosing 107 fewer acres than the second smallest, Hot Springs. Partly because of this, no one seems to find it easy to explain why it was ever declared a national park; like Hot Springs, it lacks the characteristics, the grandeur and magnificence peculiar to most of these wonderful preserves. In reality, these two parks are simply watering places to which the public goes to receive the benefits of mineral-medicinal waters. And yet, Platt has a special enchantment, the result of careful presentation of its romantic, modest attractions, appropriate to a lightly rolling terrain covered with trees, plants, and wild flowers, and dotted with springs from which streams flow and small, noisy waterfalls cascade. The lesson of Platt National Park is not devoid of value as a demonstration of what man can do to protect and preserve the qualities of nature, even when their rank is relatively humble.

*　　　*　　　*

Colorado's Rocky Mountain National Park is, because of its proximity to Denver and other cities, one of the most frequently visited and most popular of the parks. Its qualities are impressive and extraordinary. Its valleys lie 7,900 feet above sea level, but are so dominated by the surrounding peaks that the elevation is scarcely noticeable. Long's Peak reaches nearly 14,200 feet; many cliffs soar vertically from 2,200 to 3,800 feet; the park includes forty-two peaks with heights of 11,800 feet or more and nearly four miles of road at that altitude above the sea. Yet the area of the park barely exceeds 247,000 acres. It is crisscrossed by magnificent trails and by highways with easy grades that give comfortable access to passes 12,500 feet above sea level. There are many lakes, often the result of dams diligently built with admirable artistry by teams of beavers; the waters of others descend from glaciers. Quaking aspen, ponderosa pine, and ash form dense, almost impenetrable forests through which pathways wind, leading us to the wonders of a half-hundred excursions. Lodgings of all kinds abound; some guest accommodations—a rare thing in these preserves—are located on privately owned lands. All the roads in Rocky Mountain National Park are of exceptional interest for the beauty of the landscapes and the unexpected sites they lead to. But after traveling over them and noting everything of an abrupt and sensational nature that they have to show, the visitor may well remember with most affection the majestic sweetness of Bear Lake and the green hue of its smooth waters as they reflect the outline of the surrounding sierra.

*　　　*　　　*

The establishment of Sequoia National Park in 1890 guaranteed the preservation of thirty-two superb groves of trees of the *sequoia gigantea* species, the oldest and most massive trees in the world.

On summer nights, campfire talks draw large audiences in all the national parks.

Without the wise legislative provision that created this park, the colossi that inhabit it and overwhelm all who see them would have vanished long since, victims of ax and dynamite. These trees present an unforgettable spectacle, at once majestic and moving when one reflects that many of them—such as the tree named after General Sherman, with its height of 270 feet, its diameter of thirty-six feet, and its circumference at the base of nearly 100 feet (each of these dimensions exceeded by one or more of its forest companions) —have lived for more than 3,500 years and may live some centuries longer. They are enormous, but not monstrous, for what impresses one most is the beauty and harmony of their incomparable lines. In California they grow at altitudes of from 4,000 to 8,000 feet. They owe their unequaled longevity to the hardness of their wood, which is protected by a tanin-impregnated bark sometimes more than three feet thick. The first white men to venture near the region where these trees grow heard of them from the Indians, who gave an idea of their dimensions by saying that they were "like one hundred men," meaning that it would take one hundred men with fingers touching to reach around one of them. The surrounding territory adequately complements their beauty: the magnificent Sierra Nevada extends its crests and the gray, green, and white tonalities of its rocks, forests, and snow-covered peaks from the dun-covered hills of the San Joaquin Valley—the most fertile in California—to the imposing peak of Mount Whitney, which, lifting its crest 14,495 feet toward infinity from sea level, is the highest point in the continental United States outside Alaska.

*   *   *

The principal features of Shenandoah National Park can be appreciated from the highway that traverses it from north to south for a stretch of over 105 miles. If this highway, known as the Skyline Drive, did not form the basic artery of travel through a magnificent national preserve, we might say that it is cared for as if it were, in itself, a national park, so admirably is it kept and maintained. It begins at Front Royal, seventy miles from Washington, D.C., runs for most of its length through the Blue Ridge Mountains of Virginia, and ends at Rockfish Gap, near Waynesboro. Those who travel over it are offered endless opportunities to admire a succession of beautiful panoramas. At frequent intervals strategic lookouts face the distant horizon. From the Crescent Rock Overlook one obtains the best view of Hawksbill Mountain, some 4,000 feet in height. In the forests that cover the slopes are chestnuts, walnuts, pines, and lindens; wild flowers abound in spring and summer, and the variety of birds and animals is great. The proximity of such large cities as Richmond, Washington, Baltimore, Philadelphia, Pittsburgh, and New York—from which its enchantments may be reached in a single day—tends to popularize its attractions. Nearby there are ample facilities for lodgings and meals. Inside the preserve, well-marked trails penetrate or even dominate the forests, allowing the hiker to enjoy superb views of remote regions situated east or west of the park.

*   *   *

Virgin Islands National Park, astride the Atlantic and the Caribbean, owes its name to Christopher Columbus: during his second voyage to America, he christened in honor of St. Ursula and her eleven thousand virgins the archipelago of which it is part. It owes its existence as a United States preserve to the generosity of Lau-

73

rance S. Rockefeller, grandson of the elder John D. Rockefeller. In 1956, so that a national park might be established here, he gave to the government and the people of the United States some 5,000 acres owned by him on the island of St. John, that being the English version of the patronymic (San Juan) given to the island by the Spaniards. The Spaniards also christened such other islands in the archipelago as St. Thomas (Santo Tomás), St. Croix (Santa Cruz), and Tórtola (which means turtle-dove). This park is, therefore, next to the newest of the thirty national parks in the United States and its possessions. It is still not completely organized, and lacks the highway that will eventually encircle it and the facilities and services that have proved so useful in similar preserves. After 1493, the island of San Juan was occupied by Dutchmen, Englishmen, Spaniards, Frenchmen, and Danes. The Danes burned down the millennial forests that covered the island, their purpose being to plant sugar cane. Consequently, the existing trees are generally little more than a century old, but a few survivors of the fire astonish by their great size as they rise with others in dense, almost impenetrable thickets, surrounded by coconut palms and wild flowers. Impressive panoramas can be seen from heights, which, though not above 1,300 feet, offer vistas of incomparable beauty over bluffs, coves, and green islets in an alternately emerald and deep blue sea. The park's beaches are magnificent, of the finest white sand, bathed by transparent waters and bordered by royal palms. The island of St. John has 750 inhabitants; with 748 fewer, it would be an earthly paradise.

*   *   *

Lake Haiyaha Trail, which winds its way below Hallett Peak, is only one of the countless trails which in Rocky Mountain National Park lead the visitor to small or large lakes, usually surrounded by tall mountains.

Wind Cave National Park, South Dakota, in some ways resembles Kentucky's Mammoth Cave. Both are caves; both lack the qualities that usually distinguish national parks. Wind Cave owes its name to the current of air that blows into it from outside when the barometer falls and out from it when the barometer rises. Its galleries have been explored for about ten miles; it contains neither stalactites nor stalagmites, but is rich in limestone formations of curious shape called "boxwork," as abundant here as they are scarce elsewhere. The park spans an area of about 28,000 acres in the famous Black Hills, rolling country of little average elevation, but covered with clumps and masses of ponderosa pine, Rocky Mountain cedar, white ash, and quaking aspen, among which wander magnificent herds of bison, elk, antelope, and deer.

*   *   *

It is difficult to describe in a few words the wonders of Yellowstone National Park, located mostly in Wyoming, partly in Montana, with its 2,213,207 acres, its more than 300 miles of highway, its nearly 1,000 miles of trails, and its 3,000 geysers of thermal water. Yellowstone is both the oldest and the largest of the national parks. It was created in 1872 as a result of a memorandum submitted by members of the Washburn Expedition, who, after exploring it two years earlier, had confirmed reports that this territory contained unique beauties worthy of being preserved at any cost. Of all that the foresight of these men saved for us, what stands out chiefly are the valleys of the Madison, the Gibbon, and the Firehole, three trout streams of happy waters and varied landscape; the view of the Lower Falls of the Yellowstone River from Artist's Point in the imposing canyon that gives the park its name; and the steadfastness and spectacularity of Old Faithful, the most famous of geysers, which at intervals of approximately an hour and with a punctuality that justifies its name, discharges some 13,000 gallons of water, which spouts, almost boiling, at a temperature of about 205° Fahrenheit, and in winter falls frozen to the ground. The column formed by the geyser reaches about 130 feet, affording onlookers a stirring vision of great beauty.

* * *

Yosemite Valley, in California, forms one of the most nearly complete and perfect national parks imaginable. Within its great area of 757,617 acres are smiling meadows in which bright-colored, remarkably tame birds allow men to approach within a few steps of the spots where they sing, peck in the grass, and drive off their rivals; groves and forests; lakes and rivers; silky or thundering cascades, of which eight—one of them with a vertical fall of about 1,650 feet—are among the fifty most notable in the world; enormous granitic outcroppings such as Half Orange and others in the form of domes, including El Capitan, said to be the largest of its sort; fantastic outlooks; abundant, varied animal life; comfortable places in which to stay. All this in the very heart of California, a privileged land at the feet of a sierra whose gentle silhouettes delimit the horizon. When our desire for greenery and shade seems to have been satisfied by manzanita and buckthorn, various varieties of pine, live oak, cedar, and birch, we can enter Mariposa Grove and feel a new emotion before the most famous tree in the park, a giant sequoia with a diameter of about twenty-seven feet, a circumference at the base of about ninety-five feet, and a height (others are taller) of about 206 feet. Its age is calculated at about 3,800 years.

77

*   *   *

Zion National Park, near Bryce Canyon National Park but entirely distinct from it, and differing too from nearby Cedar Breaks National Monument, is located, like the other two preserves, in Utah. It is another orgy of colors in a canyon that narrows progressively, with immense rocky walls rising some 3,300 feet above its floor. The canyon was formed by the seas and rivers that inundated the region millions of years ago, depositing gravel, sand, and mud that later were converted into rock by the sheer weight of the upper layers of earth and stone. Volcanic forces, breaking through the crust of the earth, raised these rocky masses to altitudes of nearly 10,000 feet above sea level. The erosion caused by the Virgin River —which today, running some 5,000 feet below the level at which it once ran, carries off a yearly total of about 3 million tons of sediment and pulverized rock—produced the marvels that we so greatly admire in the graceful cliffs of this canyon, from which the park took its name, and revealed tonalities that range from white through red to vermillion, from blue to orange, in contrast with the greens of the poplars, maples, and willows that grow on the banks of the river and the branches of the pinyon pines and junipers that stand silhouetted against the sky along the crests of the surrounding heights.

*   *   *

It would be unfair to the prodigious work carried out by the National Park Service if, before concluding this brief description of some of the preserves entrusted to its care, no reference were made to the incomparable road known as the Blue Ridge Parkway, which

Thanks to the national park that now comprises a large part of its territory, the charm of St. John's, one of the Virgin Islands, has been preserved for future generations.

stretches for some 465 miles between Shenandoah National Park and Great Smoky Mountains National Park. A "parkway," in this case at least, is a communications route that is neither a highway nor a throughway, but excludes commercial vehicles and prohibits excessive speeds, a road planned and constructed for use by those who especially want to admire the marvels of nature during the course of a long, unhurried drive. It contains no dangerous intersections, billboards, stands selling drinks and food, or gasoline stations, and does not run through or to housing developments, towns or villages, or accommodations of any sort. It is merely a paved road, perfect for two-way traffic, its two lanes separated by a continuous white line. It has lookouts at frequent intervals which render it easy to stop and take in the beauty of the panoramas and superb landscapes that unroll like an endless ribbon before our astonished, grateful eyes. In autumn, when the trees of the Blue Ridge Mountains—which the parkway crosses at an average altitude of 3,300 feet—take on their reds and yellows, the spectacle outstrips imagination. Neither elsewhere in the United States nor in any other country is there anything that I know of comparable to the Blue Ridge Parkway. As a prolongation of the Shenandoah highway, it offers the traveler a means of communication unique in the world. When it is completed, its total length will be about 625 miles.

*　　*　　*

The National Park Service is also in charge of other similar roads: the George Washington Memorial Parkway, which eventually will measure fifty miles and runs from Mount Vernon, in Virginia near Washington, to the fort of that name in neighboring Maryland; and the Natchez Trace Parkway, approximately 205 miles long, now partially under construction, which stretches between Nashville, Tennessee, and Natchez, Mississippi.

4

Other Preserves
in the United States

I<small>N ADDITION</small> to the national parks, there exist in the United States numerous other preserves, many of them also administered by the National Park Service. The interest and importance of some of these areas and sites justify a brief catalogue of them:

1. *National Historical Parks.* These eight parks were created to preserve and commemorate episodes or relics of national history, such as the cabin in which Abraham Lincoln is supposed to have been born, battlefields, etc.

2. *National Monuments.* Official statistics place the number of national monuments at eighty-three, but the distinction between some of them and the national historical parks is occasionally not quite clear. Sometimes their determining characteristics are natural

features of terrain or landscape, but in others the chief interest seems to be archaeological, geological, historical, or military. Some of the national monuments recall Spanish activities within the present United States during the sixteenth, seventeenth, eighteenth, and even nineteenth centuries; I shall refer to these in some detail later on (see Appendix, page 96).

3. *National Military Parks.* These eleven sites commemorate sieges of forts or cities, battles, victories, etc.

4. *National Battlefields.* These signalize military episodes of the Civil War.

5. *National Memorial Park.* The only site in this category is dedicated to the memory of President Theodore Roosevelt.

6. *National Battlefield Sites.* The descriptive name given to these five sites defines them without differentiating their characteristics from those of the national battlefields (paragraph 4).

7. *National Historic Sites.* These ten sites commemorate events and features of very diverse interest: political, architectural, military, etc.

8. *National Memorials.* Usually these honor some great national figure. Of the twelve in existence, five are in Washington, D. C.

9. *National Parkways.* Three exist (all are mentioned above), and all are of great beauty or historic interest.

10. *National Cemeteries.* These are ten. They were established between 1862 and 1866 for the burial of those who fell in the Civil War.

11. *National Capital Parks.* These urban parks, created in 1790, embellish Washington, D.C.

12. *National Recreation Areas.* There are four of these—three lakes and the immense Grand Coulee Dam Reservoir—which are open to the public for purely recreational purposes.

13. *National Historic Sites.* Unlike the sites mentioned above (paragraph 7), these do not belong to the United States government. They are eight, and they are of comparable interest.

14. *National Seashore Recreational Area.* There is one, at Cape Hatteras, North Carolina.

15. *National Forests.* These exist in thirty-seven states and in Puerto Rico. They cover a total area of about 181 million acres (greater than that of the national parks). Through them run some 70,000 miles of streams and rivers. They contain thousands of lakes and ponds and thousands of miles of trails for hikers and horseback riders. They are open to the public for all kinds of sports, notably winter sports, mountain climbing, fishing, and hunting. Fishing and hunting are permitted except in zones classified as refuges; elsewhere they are subject to the laws of the state in which the area lies. Accommodations of all sorts abound in the national forests; with few exceptions, these establishments belong to private individuals and are administered and managed privately. The national forests are under the jurisdiction of the Forest Service of the Department of Agriculture. They are superb preserves, comparable to national parks, and the public takes full advantage of them for entertainment and relaxation.

16. *National Trails.* These trails, of which there are two, the Appalachian Trail and the Pacific Crest Trail, respectively about 2,000 and 2,300 miles in length, wind through the mountain ranges

83

along the eastern seaboard and the west coast. Both are of prime interest and beauty. Together, they traverse twenty-seven national forests and eight national parks.

17. *Indian Reservations.* Some of these very numerous areas are enormous—that of the Navajos in Arizona and New Mexico is three times as large as Massachusetts. They are reserved in accord with treaties made with the Indian tribes who have lived in these areas since primitive times. The Indians are not forced to live on them; many of them prefer to live in other localities, like anyone else in the United States. On the reservations, however, they may avail themselves of certain free services and assistance. Their traditional festivals are notable; celebrated at stated times of the year on many reservations, they attract large numbers of visitors.

18. *National Wildlife Refuges.* About 300 of these exist in the United States and Puerto Rico. All together they cover an enormous territory—a total of about 18 million acres which come under the jurisdiction of the Fish and Animal Life Service of the Department of the Interior. By supplying the rivers and lakes with game fish in sufficient numbers for sportsmen, and by protecting the national fauna, this Service contributes extraordinarily to the increase and regulated use of the resources in question. Edifying and exemplary results have been achieved in the few years that have elapsed since the foundation of the Service, which was created by combining two bureaus already in existence. Thanks to it, and partly as the result of close, intelligent collaboration between United States and Canadian officials—and despite the 14 million individual hunting licenses granted annually—there are now in unprotected areas, provided the season is good, more wild ducks and geese than ever. The number of deer taken annually in open country by hunters with suitable rifles, unlimited ammunition, and all the automobiles imagin-

Of all the wonders of nature in the thirty national parks, Old Faithful, in Yellowstone, draws the largest number of visitors—as many as one million people during the brief summer season.

able is calculated at 1.5 million. The refuges have ample facilities for meals during daylight hours, but no overnight accommodations. Fishing is permitted, but both hunting and camping are prohibited. Of great interest are the measures taken jointly by the United States and Canada to protect the variety of heron known as the whooping crane. Few of these birds survive, and the species is in danger of extinction. But thanks to recent steps to protect them—steps in which the United States Air Force co-operated by renouncing a zone useful for its experimental flights and shooting—the whooping cranes have begun to increase in number. Most recent seasons have registered a higher number of births than in the preceding years.

19. *Reservoirs and Dams.* These hydraulic works, aside from the practical uses to which they are put, can be compared to natural lakes inasmuch as they serve as nurseries for fish and aquatic birds. They are also utilized for various sports. For these reasons, they are entrusted to the care of the same government agency that looks after the national wildlife refuges mentioned in paragraph 18.

20. *State Parks and Recreational Areas.* These are preserves set aside by the various states; the Federal government does not administer them. But their huge total area—approximately 7.4 million acres—contributes, apart from their obvious interest, to their extraordinary importance. They may be classified as state parks, state forests, recreational zones properly speaking, and historic sites. Many of them have accommodations of various kinds as well as facilities for camping, fishing, boating, horseback riding, etc. They exist in all the states and are a source of pride to the people. Their locations and entrances are clearly marked along roads that pass near them.

What Has Been Done in the United States

*   *   *

Such, in brief, is what the United States has done to safeguard nature and attest to its inestimable value before all, while commemorating historical facts that are part of every man's heritage. It is not easy to find in other countries endeavors at once so civilized and so civilizing which surpass these. What has been achieved here clearly reflects the high degree of culture of those who inspired and carried out these projects, and it transcends the aims, already described above, to serve which the preserves were primarily set aside.

In the following pages I shall examine these projects and attempt to determine how the lessons taught here can be applied by other nations.

WHAT HAS BEEN DONE IN THE UNITED STATES;
WHAT OTHER COUNTRIES CAN DO

In the countries of Central and South America, and in the Caribbean as well as in Spain—and I mention Spain not only because it is my country, but also because it is closely related to the areas I have just named—opportunities exist to develop a program patterned after the one so successfully implemented in the United States, with due provision for varying factors and in keeping with the dictates of common sense. Let us examine these opportunities and at the same time see whether we find sufficient argument to justify action.

Spain and the nations of Central and South America and the Caribbean possess vast natural resources, some of which now need protection for their adequate preservation. It is worthwhile to inquire whether they could follow the lines drawn toward this end by the United States and Canada. Clearly, I do not refer either to the size of the preserves or to the fabulous degree of organization and

87

perfection reached in many of them. I refer simply to the urgent need of converting certain areas into national trusts compelling pride and admiration and stimulating local and foreign tourism. Nature has been generous to these lands. If they would take advantage of their vast potentialities, the results would be not only astonishing but also highly productive. Adequate accesses and roads—well surfaced to do away with clouds of dust—the posting of clear directions wherever required; facilities comparable to those which exist in the national parks of the United States; the protection and defense of the flora and fauna; lookouts provided with orientation tables and the intelligible information, to make intelligent looking possible; trails and pathways. At least a minimal interpretative service, with talks, libraries, and small museums. Well-organized prevention of fires, accidents, and other calamities; regulated fishing for sportsmen; absolute permanent prohibition of hunting except in areas comparable to the United States national forests. Decent, clean zones for camping, as many sanitary facilities as required— and the enforced obligation to use them, imposed under threat of punishment, with fines out of proportion to the apparent lightness of possible infractions. Accommodations for varying purses and tastes, the more rustic the better, but none lacking the minimum essential comforts. Centralized services for meals of the frugal, simple sort that outdoor life calls for. Civic instruction for visitors, so that they may benefit from what they see and increase their fund of knowledge; and discreet but effective publicity consisting chiefly of colored photographs and films that can spread word of the unique attractions of the preserves far and wide, so that these enchantments may not run the risk of remaining unknown or known only to the handful but for whom they would fall into oblivion.

Practically all the countries referred to could have excellent national parks by resorting to modest but effective planning of this

Blacktail deer are frequently seen in the Yosemite Valley, at the foot of the massive Half Dome in Yosemite National Park.

sort. It would not be difficult to determine which areas qualify for the honor of being declared preserves under the custody of the nation. The ultimate decision should not rest on purely local considerations, which are likely to be irksome. It would soon become evident that certain landscapes have preserved their primitive characteristics and possess features worthy of national parks, which should be established before the indiscriminate building of highways or the exploitation of hydroelectric or forest wealth endangers flora, fauna, and timberlands.

Without wishing to suggest that other countries unreservedly copy the system now existing in the United States, I would urge that the American project be used as a model adaptable to other areas in which "progress" threatens the conservation of immensely valuable, irreplaceable natural resources, the enjoyment of which should be guaranteed to future generations.

What about history? A dozen or so of the various categories of preserves and monuments administered by the United States Department of the Interior can be grouped under one common heading —history, the fostering of respect for history.

He would be judging rashly who asserted that these monuments constitute the only tribute that Americans render to the past, apart from the memorials and inevitable statues that honor outstanding figures in almost every town. The cult of history, of the relatively brief, but already very considerable history of the United States, is an outstanding trait of the American people. True, some Americans have only the vaguest notions of their history. But it is equally true that many of them are devoted to history and help to bring it before the public by commemorating significant events. Thus, all along the extensive highways that crisscross the entire country from north to south and east to west, you will see historical markers of good size, solidly built of wood or metal, with clearly legible inscriptions in high relief. These commemorative signs recount to the passing traveler facts, some more worthy of note than others, about events that occured in the region or at the very spot where the marker stands beside the road. To give an idea of what these markers say, I quote here the text of Commemorative Stone 33 in the state of Utah, situated on Highway 91 south of Scipio, in Millard County:

> The written history of this intermountain region begins in 1776 with the remarkably accurate diary of Father Escalante, a Spanish Franciscan Priest. He and Father Dominguez, together with eight companions, were the first white men known to have been here.
>
> On a futile journey, trying to locate a direct route between Santa Fe, New Mexico, center of Catholic missionary activities, and Monterey, California, recently established port of entry for goods from Spain and Southern Mexico, they traversed most of Utah east of Salt Lake Valley. On the return journey to Santa Fe, they crossed this divide in October, 1776.
>
> The history of their wanderings over strange trails and their missionary work among Indian tribes furnishes one of the most impressive accounts of exploration, adventure and heroism in the history of the west. Their travels extended more than 1,600 miles over mountains and deserts. Without competent guides or a knowledge of the country before them, and depending only upon information and assistance from the Indians, they endured untold hardship and privation, finally reaching Santa Fe on January 2, 1777.

A history lesson like that taught by this marker makes a deep impression when learned from a stone along the road while one is traveling. One looks all around and sees the vast terrain across which, under conditions so much less comfortable than our own, walked the humble, inspired pioneer whose journeying has been thought worthy of commemoration. Thus learned, the lesson is not forgotten quickly.

The cities of the eastern United States are still too young to evoke similar memories: they lack that kind of history. On the other hand, some roads and fields show traces of the patina of time. Like the Camino Real, which stretches from the Atlantic to the Pacific, many eastern trails, once narrow and dangerous, have been converted into straight, safe, paved highways, and they constantly speak to us of the past. In the relatively old states of the east— Virginia, New York, Pennsylvania, Connecticut, Massachusetts— the cities are full of commemorative markers that refresh the memory, move wayfarers deeply, and make hearts beat a little faster.

One thinks of other nations, also replete with history, but lacking such evocations of the past. Certainly, the very stones speak eloquently of past times, but their eloquence says nothing to those who cannot read them and who therefore dismantle castles to build prosaic edifices or scribble on the walls of cathedrals and monuments. A few miles of travel along principal highways, and one passes close to fields on which decisive battles were fought. But often the traveler encounters no adequate evocations of these significant events.

THE AIMS

The spirit that first moved a handful of Americans to undertake the work of conservation summed up in the preceding pages was possibly purely scientific. The re-evaluation of nature, so matchlessly achieved in the organization of the national parks, received its first impulse from men of that sort—archaeologists, geologists, botanists, and others—who shared the pride of having discovered in their own land the existence of areas of unsurpassed beauty which had to be preserved at all costs.

With the passing of time and the development of communications, it eventually became apparent that the work accomplished had social repercussions far beyond anything that could have been foreseen at the start. The parks and the other preserves had turned out to be of interest not merely to a few people, not merely to the most cultivated and informed; they had captured the imagination of the masses who, first by thousands, later by hundreds of thousands, finally by millions, made the effort nesessary to visit them, using them as vacation and holiday centers.

Accommodations were constructed; catering arrangements were set up. Provisions were made for the exhibition and sale of handicrafts and souvenirs of every sort and origin. Public transportation underwent extraordinary development. The preserves were instrumental in placing huge sums of money in circulation, thus becoming sources of wealth to many. Their economic importance grew to immense proportions.

As this happened, the endless possibilities of the undertaking became patent. The states containing national parks began to register astronomical numbers of visitors. A good part of the ten million tourists welcomed by Canada in 1957 went to that country attracted by the natural beauties of such famous parks as Banff and Jasper. And if the number of Canadian tourists in the United States exceeded the number of visitors to Canada from the south, that was owing in no small measure to the potent attractions of the national parks of the United States—which were visited in 1961 by seventy-eight million persons, a number that makes them the

Some sequoias, such as these in Mariposa Grove, Yosemite National Park, are almost 4,000 years old.

greatest tourist attraction in the world and a fabulous source of wealth.

Given these circumstances, can it be doubted that the parks and related preserves have political importance in the United States? Veritable tempests have swirled around them—about whether or not they should be established in the first place, about the ban on exploitation of their huge mineral, agricultural, forestal, and hydroelectric resources. The zeal with which conservation is carried out, the lack of zeal in caring for a given animal species— these factors have influenced the election of senators, the political futures of governors. The conservation, survival, and continuity of the national parks could conceivably be a deciding factor even in a presidential election.

These considerations aside, the patriotism of a great people remains. To know one's country is to love it, especially when it is beautiful. In the United States, the most beautiful regions, now evaluated with singular foresight and exquisite sensitivity, are the national parks. As I pointed out at the beginning of this book, no citizen of the United States who is proud of his citizenship fails to take pride in them.

To sum up: the aims pursued in the creation of the national parks and related preserves, the interests that have spurred their development, are scientific, social, economic, touristic, and political. And let us not forget that the true appreciation of their native soil contributes to the patriotism of the people, to the love that they feel for their country.

These may be the factors that have justified the immense work carried out by the government of the United States in creating, organizing, and maintaining the parks and other preserves on so high a level and in a form so worthy of admiration.

APPENDIX

Traces of Spain

TRACES OF SPAIN IN THE NATIONAL PARKS
AND MONUMENTS OF THE UNITED STATES

Dᴜʀɪɴɢ the sixteenth, seventeenth, eighteenth, and nineteenth centuries, Spanish activity in the regions later integrated into the United States was far more intense than may people now suppose. Vestiges of that activity lie in full view. Some have tried to hide them, but others have sung their glories. To bring them back to life it is sufficient to stir up old memories.

Few relate the Spaniards in America and the national parks of the United States. Nevertheless, the connection is there. Let us begin our quest in the most remote of the forty-eight contiguous states—Washington, on the Pacific Coast, adjoining Canada—and we shall soon find traces of Spain.

Olympic National Park is a preserve as distant as any from the big cities of the Atlantic seaboard, from the geographic center of the forty-eight contiguous states, and from the nation's capital. Let us see what is said of a Spaniard on a commemorative stone in the state of Washington on the Pacific Coast, on the edge of a marvelous highway that runs close to this magnificent park:

> The Spanish captain Juan Perez sailed north from San Blas in 1774, with orders from Spain to claim the coast, against the Russians. Perez discovered Nootka Sound on the west shore of Vancouver Island and traded with the natives of the Queen Charlottes. He sighted a snow peak, towering high and afar from a rock-bound coast, on August 11, 1774. He named it Sierra Nevada de Santa Rosalia. Four years later British captain John Meares was the second explorer to observe the mighty peak. He named it Mt. Olympus.

Two captains of Coronado's troops, Pedro de Tovar and López de Cárdenas, were, in 1540, the first white men to be struck with awe before the wonders of the Grand Canyon of the Colorado, in Arizona.

The wooded heights of Great Smoky Mountains National Park were sighted by Hernando de Soto in the sixteenth century when he traveled with his men through what is now North Carolina and Tennessee.

The discovery of the Hawaiian archipelago generally is attributed to Captain James Cook of the Royal British Navy, who arrived there in 1778. But the *Haleakala Guide* published by the Hawaii Natural History Association in 1959 asserts that a Spanish navigator, Juan Gaetano, visited the islands in 1555. Contemporary documents in the Spanish Archives, the *Haleakala Guide* states, show a group of islands in the latitude of Hawaii, but ten degrees of longitude too far west. What corresponds to the island of Maui is called *La Desgraciada* (The Unfortunate); the island of Hawaii is labeled *La Mesa* (The Table); and what appears to represent Kahoolawe, Lanai, and Molokai is called *Los Monjes* (The Monks). Despite the error in the recorded longitude, the fact that the islands appear on the chart, as well as their approximate locations—there are no other islands in the vicinity—allow us to assume with some assurance that Juan Gaetano was in effect the first white man to cast his eyes on the region that now includes Haleakala and Hawaii national parks.

In 1541, De Soto was in what is now Hot Springs National Park, Arkansas.

Kings Canyon, California, owes its name to the Spaniards who discovered the river of the Holy Kings one January 6, the feast of the Three Magi, in whose honor they named the area Canyon of the Three Kings.

Mesa Verde, Colorado, was discovered by Juan María de Rivera in 1765. Ten years later, Father Escalante camped near what is now the entrance to Mesa Verde National Park.

The Olympic Mountains, dominating the Strait of Juan de Fuca from the state of Washington and forming the central spine of Olympic National Park, were discovered in 1774 by a lieutenant of the Spanish navy, Juan Pérez, who named the highest of them Cerro de Santa Rosalía. Four years later an English navigator, John Meares, saw the same peak from the Strait of Juan de Fuca and gave it the name of Mount Olympus, which has been used ever since on maps and maritime charts.

Platt National Park, Oklahoma, is a part of the territory that was traversed by Coronado's captains in or about 1542, when they were exploring the southern part of what is now the United States.

At least some of the seventy-five peaks that rise above 9,800 feet in Rocky Mountain National Park were sighted by Father Silvestre Vélez de Escalante, Father Francisco Atanasio Domínguez, and Captain Miera y Pacheco, who accompanied the priests during their fabulous wanderings through what now is Colorado.

The men who discovered Kings Canyon and the River of the Holy Kings were the first to know or to hear anything about the gigantic trees that grow in Sequoia National Park, California.

The island of St. John, where Virgin Islands National Park is now established, was christened San Juan in 1493 by Christopher Columbus.

The discovery of the area known today as Yosemite National Park, in California, is generally attributed to two American explorers. But this marvelous region is full of Spanish names—the Merced River, Mariposa Grove, El Mono and Fernández passes, El Portal, El Capitan—an indication that the first men to become acquainted with its principal features spoke Spanish.

Zion, in Utah, forms part of the territories crossed by Father Escalante and his companions in 1776 during their march from Santa Fe into Colorado and Utah and back in search of the best route for reaching the missions that other Franciscan fathers had established on the coast of California.

Spaniards did not discover Mount McKinley or the region of Alaska that now constitute the magnificent park bearing its name, but they were relatively close to these areas in the course of the expeditions which, for political reasons, they carried out from Acapulco by order of Charles III during the last third of the seventeenth century. Abundant traces remain of their passage along the southern coasts of Alaska. I myself have counted, on the spot or on recently published maps, some two hundred Spanish place names— towns such as Valdes and Cordova, capes, promontories, mountains, bays, creeks, islands, lakes, and rivers—which have endured for nearly two centuries. Spaniards, therefore, were not only the first Europeans to visit vast areas of Central and South America and of the continental United States, but also the first to explore and occupy part of Alaska, passing its western confines and anchoring their ships among the Aleutian Islands.

In the museum at Hot Springs National Park, Arkansas, the Park Service, whose leaflets are the source for some of the preceding data, commemorates the Spanish discoveries in America with these words:

> Spain implanted her religion and culture in a New World nearly a century before other European nations gained a foothold inside it. A few courageous soldiers, priests and colonists spread Spanish Dominions from Arkansas to Peru and left a heritage of culture which still flourishes in the South West and in countries south of the United States. De Soto ranks with Pizarro and Cortés amongst the great conquistadores. Although his last expedition failed, it explored 4,000 miles of wilderness and traversed the territories occupied by ten States of the Union.

*   *   *

Eleven national monuments or historic sites in the custody of the National Park Service are linked to Spanish activities in the United States and one of its dependencies.

1. De Soto National Memorial, in Bradenton, Florida, commemorates the Conquistador's prodigious march through unexplored and inhospitable regions. It lasted four years, during

which De Soto journeyed with his men through more than 4,000 miles of forest and wilderness.

The National Park Service's leaflet on this monument—an evocative, simple, and romantic area of some fifty acres situated at the entrance to Tampa Bay—is dedicated entirely to the personality of Hernando de Soto and to his prodigious, well-organized expedition through virgin territories. "Don Hernando de Soto," the leaflet says, "caballero de Santiago and a gentleman by all four descents, was a typical conquistador. Charles V appointed him Governor of Cuba and Adelantado (leader) to 'conquer, pacify, and populate' the northern continent.

"On April 17, 1538, trumpets sounded and cannon thundered as the flotilla left San Lúcar, Spain, with about 700 volunteers aboard. The winds were favorable, and De Soto's bride was at his side.

"In Havana, on May 18, 1539, De Soto bade farewell to his Doña Isabel and set sail for Florida. On May 30, the army landed on the west coast, apparently at Tampa Bay. A few ruined pearls lay in the dust at the deserted Indian village where they camped, and the Spaniards believed themselves at the threshold of fortune. So Narváez had thought, when he chanced upon a single golden ornament!

"Spanish scouts found the lost Juan Ortiz, who had come to Florida with Narváez and had been saved by a native princess from death at the stake. For 10 years Ortiz had been a slave of the Indians, and, while he had seen no riches, he had heard wonderful reports of the interior land. De Soto assigned 100 men to guard the camp and sent the ships back to Cuba for supplies. The march through 4,000 miles of unknown land began on July 15, 1539.

"De Soto led 600 or more disciplined veterans who averaged—and sometimes doubled—a steady 10 miles a day on the march. Counting the Indians drafted as they went along, the expedition must often have numbered up to 1,000 people. About 200 horses mounted the lancers. There were about 300 crossbowmen and harquebusiers, a dozen priests, a physician, and workmen to build boats and bridges or repair weapons and rivet the slave chains.

"As they pushed northward, heat and hunger plagued them; hidden natives rained arrows upon them. De Soto followed the practice of seizing village chieftains and forcing them to supply food, carriers, and guides. Once beyond Ocale (in what is now Florida), Indians gathered to rescue their chief, but the Spaniards moved first, driving the warriors into nearby lakes.

"De Soto continued onward. Then from winter quarters in the hostile Apalachee farmlands (now northern Florida, near Apalachee Bay), he summoned the men left at the landing site, while to Havana he sent a present of 20 Indian women for Doña Isabel. Meanwhile, his scouts discovered Pensacola Bay; others saw the bleached bones of Narváez' horses at Apalachee Bay.

"In the spring of 1540, they marched toward the Savannah River, where the comely chieftainess of the Cofitachequi, an Indian village, bestowed her pearl necklace upon Don Hernando. Another 200 pounds of pearls were dug from the burial mounds. But the Adelantado pushed onward. If no richer land were found, they could always return.

"Some were lame and sick by the time they reached a region called Xuala in what is now western South Carolina, but here they saw 'more indications of gold mines than in all the country they had traversed.' Up into what is now North Carolina, then across the Smokies into Tennessee they went. Mulberries, nuts, maize, and turkeys the natives gave willingly, as the army pressed southward toward 'Coosa' in central Alabama, still searching for treasure.

"Powerful Tuscalusa, lord of the Mobile Indians, hid his anger when the Spainiards seized him, and agreed to furnish 400 carriers as soon as they reached the town of 'Mabila.' But warriors—not carriers—surrounded De Soto in Mabila. The Spaniards fought free and in a fierce day-long battle burned the Indian town and slaughtered 3,000 Indians. De Soto suffered crippling losses in this battle; 20 men killed, including a brother-in-law and a nephew; a number of horses killed; most of the expedition's supplies and property destroyed; 'and the wounded comprised all the men of most worth and honor in the army.'

"De Soto had planned to meet supply ships on the coast and send the pearls of Cofitachequi to Havana. But the pearls were lost at Mabila. Some of his disillusioned men, naked under their rusty mail, planned to sail with the ships. To prevent this, De Soto again turned his face from the coast.

"The expedition almost ended in the spring of 1541, when the Chickasaw Indians made a surprise dawn attack on the northern Mississippi camp. Fortunately, the Indians mistook stampeding horses for cavalry and withdrew; yet a dozen Spaniards lost their lives, and 50 horses were killed. Clothing, saddles, and weapons were burned. Shaking with cold, the men covered themselves with grass mats, while they fashioned new saddles and lances.

"On May 8, 1541, De Soto saw 'the great River,' so wide that 'if a man stood still on the other side, it could not be discerned whether he were a man or no.' Beyond the Mississippi lay the rumored wealth of Pacaha Province, so the artisans built barges and the army crossed for the march into Arkansas to the mouth of the St. Francis. Finding no gold, they turned west, then south, to winter on the west bank of the Ouachita River, near what is now Camden, Ark. Here, the interpreter Juan Ortiz died, a great loss.

"Even De Soto was discouraged. He went back to the Mississippi, plainning to settle at a seaport and refit for a westward advance, but the scouts found no news of the sea. To terrorize the populous country and keep the Indians from uniting against him, De Soto ordered the destruction of the Anilco village in what is now Louisiana. The fighting was left to his lieutenants, for De Soto, called by his men 'one of the best lances who have passed to the New World,' was burning with fever. A few days later, on May 21, 1542, Hernando De Soto died.

"Not all mourned his passing, for he was a stern man. Yet, his skill and courage demanded respect, and his concern for his men won devotion. Secretly, they buried their knight within the village walls, telling the Indians that the 'Child of the Sun' had ascended to his father. When the natives saw the loosened earth and whispered, the Spaniards dug up the body, weighted it in an oaken casket, and sank it in the dark bosom of the Father of Waters, as the Indians called the Mississippi."

2.   Fort Caroline, Florida, is a commemorative monument principally related to the passage of the French through this region. It also signalizes Spanish military actions; for that reason I include it here.

3.   Fort Frederica National Monument, in Georgia, commemorates the struggles among Spain, France, and England for possession of this region.

4.   The Fort of Matanzas, a national monument, is a small fortress not far from St. Augustine, Florida. Protected by this fort, the Spaniards here destroyed the French who threatened them.

5.   Castillo de San Marcos National Monument, Florida, is an impressive fortress in classic style, built by the Spaniards in St. Augustine to defend the city and protect the ships that sailed along the Gulf Stream on their way to and from Mexico, loaded with merchandise and traveling between Spanish and Caribbean ports while exposed to the attacks of English pirates. In this fortress, since

November 9, 1955, the flag of Spain again flies alongside the flag of the United States.

6.   San Juan National Historic Site, in Puerto Rico, consists of fortifications, walls, and buildings constructed by the Spaniards.

7.   Cabrillo National Monument, in California, commemorates the discovery of the Bay of San Diego by the Portuguese Juan Rodríguez Cabrillo, a member of a Spanish expedition in 1542.

8.   El Morro National Monument, in New Mexico, covers an area of some 250 acres. It was declared a national monument in 1906 to preserve the inscriptions by Spanish and other explorers on its rocky walls.

9.   Gran Quivira National Monument, New Mexico, was a Spanish mission during the seventeenth century.

10.   Tumacacori National Monument, Arizona, commemorates another Spanish mission.

11.   Finally, San Jose Mission National Historic Site, Texas, jointly administered by the Catholic Church and the state of Texas, was designed to preserve one of the numerous missions established in the United States by Spaniards.

*   *   *

It is thus that the memory of Spain's ventures—exploratory, military, or spiritual, always heroic in the face of peril—is honored in areas that now form part of the United States and its possessions. This tradition provides a treasury of resources which, through Spanish and American public opinion, can help to cement Spain's close relations with a country to which so many peoples are linked today by close friendship.

Index

A NOTE ABOUT THE AUTHOR

Luis A. Bolin was born in Málaga, Spain, and was educated at the universities of Granada and Madrid and also studied at Middle Temple, London. He has been war correspondent, press attaché with the Spanish Embassy in London, member of the Information Section of the League of Nations, and director general of the Spanish National Tourist Department. Mr. Bolin has traveled widely in Europe and in the Americas. His travels include personal visits to all thirty of the national parks in the United States; he is also familiar with other national parks in Spain and Canada. For fifteen years he had under his care two national big-game preserves in Spain. Mr. Bolin, who was awarded the Grand Cross of the Order of Civil Merit in Spain, is at present vice-chairman of the European Travel Commission and information counselor with the Spanish Embassy in Washington, D.C.

March 1962

A NOTE ON THE TYPE

THE TEXT of this book is set in CALEDONIA, a Linotype face designed by W. A. Dwiggins (1880–1956), the man responsible for so much that is good in contemporary book design and typography. Caledonia belongs to the family of printing types called "modern face" by printers—a term used to mark the change in style of type-letters which occurred about 1800. Caledonia borders on the general design of Scotch Modern but is more freely drawn than that letter.

Composed by Brown Brothers Linotypers, New York.
Printed by the Murray Printing Company,
Forge Village, Mass.
Bound by H. Wolff, New York.
Typography and binding design by
VINCENT TORRE